CONFIDENCE

MAGNETISM

KNOW YOUR VALUE

SHOW YOUR VALUE

CHARISMA

SEE OTHERS' VALUE

CONNECTION

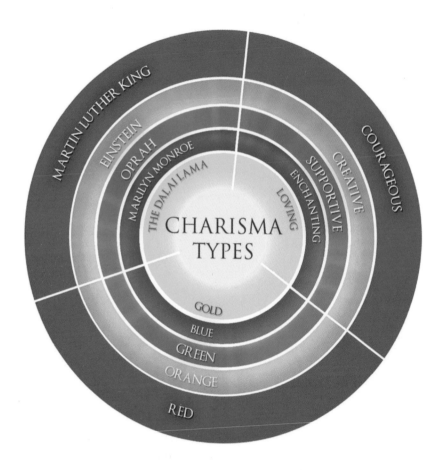

CHARISMA TYPES

MARTIN LUTHER KING
EINSTEIN
OPRAH
MARILYN MONROE
THE DALAI LAMA
LOVING
ENCHANTING
SUPPORTIVE
CREATIVE
COURAGEOUS

GOLD
BLUE
GREEN
ORANGE
RED

* The individuals pictured as the five Charisma Types are for informational purposes only.
They represent no endorsement of any product or idea mentioned by the author.

"This book is an abracadabra entrance into the inner sanctum of charisma! The information shared is pertinent to performers wishing to court audiences as well as those simply looking to court the mysteries of their hearts."

–Jeff McBride, creator of the Magic & Mystery School, Guinness World Record Holder and World Ambassador of Magic

"I have visited 42 countries in my life as a performer, and as a global citizen. I have observed that there is a language of connectedness human beings share just by being human. It exists in a place where spoken words do not. Communication is the key to global peace and harmony. Robin Sol Lieberman and *The Charisma Code* tap into this powerful truth."

–Durga McBroom, singer for Pink Floyd and Blue Pearl

"Most people who seek out therapy often suffer from lack of confidence. It is the result of distorted thinking developed over time by one's upbringing, negative experiences, and environment. In *The Charisma Code*, the inspirational Robin Sol Lieberman addresses the very notion of how to develop a positive view of the self."

–Ruzanna Avetisyan, Licensed Marriage and Family Therapist

"I highly recommend *The Charisma Code*. You will discover which type of leader you are and how to emerge as a global citizen. Robin reminds us to listen to our heart, our soul, and our intuition. Her book is an honest invitation to live into Greatness."

–Amandine Roche, UN Human Rights expert, author, and founder of Amanuddin Foundation

"*The Charisma Code* is a powerful tool to enhance your self care, both psychologically and physically."

–Scott Kuhagen, creator of M11Fitness® & M11Restorative Techniques®

"Charisma is a key to influence. Influence is a key to success. And *The Charisma Code* is a key to having the life you want."

–Stephen Shapiro, Hall of Fame speaker and author of *Best Practices Are Stupid*

THE
CHARISMA CODE

THE
CHARISMA CODE
COMMUNICATING IN A LANGUAGE BEYOND WORDS

ROBIN SOL LIEBERMAN

WHITE CLOUD PRESS
ASHLAND, OREGON

White Cloud Press books may be purchased for educational,
business, or sales promotional use. For information, please write:
Special Market Department, White Cloud Press,
PO Box 3400, Ashland, OR 97520
www.whitecloudpress.com

Front cover and back cover photographs © 2016 by Michele Zousmer.
Back page photography by Clay Patrick McBride and Starla Fortunato.
Interior author photo by Patrick Bastien.
Cover and Interior Design by Christy Collins, C Book Services
and Lieve Maas, Bright Light Graphics

Printed in the United States
First edition: 2016
16 17 18 19 20   10 9 8 7 6 5 4 3 2 1

Library of Congress Cataloging-in-Publication Data

Names: Lieberman, Robin Sol, author.
Title: The charisma code : communicating in a language beyond words
/ by Robin Sol Lieberman.
Description: First edition. | Ashland, Oregon : White Cloud Press, [2016] |
Includes bibliographical references and index.
Identifiers: LCCN 2015046280 | ISBN 9781940468402 (paperback)
Subjects: LCSH: Charisma (Personality trait) | Interpersonal relations. |
Interpersonal communication. | BISAC: BUSINESS & ECONOMICS /
Leadership.
Classification: LCC BF698.35.C45 L45 2016 | DDC 153.6--dc23
LC record available at http://lccn.loc.gov/2015046280

To my mother and father,
each the revolutionary:
You have always encouraged me
to follow my heart.

CONTENTS

FOREWORD

I sign each of my emails with the following:

To cherish humanity over nationhood;
I am, a citizen of the world.

JANET C. SALAZAR

Born in the Philippines, I now work from the United Nations Headquarters in New York City. When I met Robin Sol Lieberman, I saw a lifelong ally as passionately driven as I am, using *The Charisma Code* teachings to help elevate the emerging culture of the global citizen, and inspire each individual to live in their Greatness.

I first met Robin in May of 2015. My soul friend, Naila Chowdhury, had invited me to join her at the Joan B. Kroc Institute for Peace and Justice at the University of San Diego, California for a microfinance summit. I knew little about microfinance, but Naila, having worked for fifteen years alongside Nobel Peace Laureate and Father of Microfinance, Muhammad Yunnus, is walking testimony to its ability to unlock the power of the world's poorest billions. When Naila asked me to fly to San Diego for this summit, something inside nudged me to say yes, and I followed the nudge.

I would soon learn that this kind of obedience is a key tenet of *The Charisma Code*. It means you listen to your heart, your soul, your God, your intuition. You listen to whatever you trust the most, and you follow. This was a language I loved, a language I lived, but I didn't know it yet.

A few days later, there I was at the breathtaking, most beautiful campus I have ever seen, sitting atop a hill overlooking the entire San Diego landscape and the Pacific Ocean. The Joan B.

Kroc Institute for Peace and Justice: the perfect location to forge a new revolutionary alliance.

That night, when the summit ended, Naila and I lingered in the hallway with a few other ladies, all of us inspired and exhausted. And then she came. Robin Sol Lieberman, looking like the rising sun, radiant with warmth and enthusiasm. I liked her immediately. Before we parted for some much needed slumber, Robin handed me a copy of *The Charisma Code*. Back in my room, tired as I was, and with eyes begging me to give them a break, I couldn't put the book down without at least taking a peek. I decided to read the first few pages. The inspiration was instant! Aha moments flew like fireworks. The fable of the "Stone Soup" story in Chapter One jumped out, affirming the essence of the Power of Collaboration. I was hooked. I sat up and delved in, putting both pen and highlighter to work. New thoughts, vital thoughts, thoughts worth asking questions about! I felt Life energies jump out from each page straight into my heart, my brain, my innermost thought and realization chambers. *Vita!*

I call this book "the catalyst for genuine human connection." It doesn't matter what country or neighborhood you find yourself in; when you learn to speak charisma code, you surpass barriers of language, nationhood, politics, religion, and dress and instead establish genuine connection. As the following story demonstrates, Robin can connect with anyone. She is the embodiment of true charisma.

After an event in Los Angeles with Amma, the Hugging Saint, Robin and I were hanging out with Twyla Garrett, who'd beaten the odds of growing up as a black American in extreme poverty and domestic violence to become the author of *Homeland Security* and the President and CEO of IME, a multi-million grossing firm. The three of us were hungry. Our hosts provided delicious vegetarian fare, but Twyla, without a sweat bead of shame, asked for red meat.

In the car and busting out laughing, Robin told Twyla, "Girl, you are the embodiment of *The Charisma Code*'s Step One: Confidence. You know who you are, you know your value, and you're not afraid to be different from those around you."

Twyla replied, "I've been hugging a saint all day; now I need my meat. It's just what is."

Robin would only eat meat that had "lived a happy life," so we ruled out all fast food and decided on Mexican fare. I got busy asking Yelp to lead us to the nearest restaurant. Three miles later, we heard Mariachi music blasting from backyards surrounded by barbed wire. As we passed a hole in the wall storefront, Robin exclaimed, "That place looks really good!"

She zipped a U-turn and parked. We climbed out of the car in our spiritual-white Amma gear and proceeded to cover our luggage with shawls. High-heeling our way down the uneven, neglected sidewalk, we entered the loudest Mexican karaoke bar I have ever been in. Even on a Sunday night, the place was packed. Packed with people and packed with pitchers of margaritas, tortilla chips, and beer bottles. I turned to Twyla.

"I don't think we're in Kansas anymore."

Hardly able to hear each other's words under the Spanish lyrics belted out by a dark, big-bellied, handlebar-mustached man, the three of us huddled together while this restaurant full of Mexicans, loudly living their culture, stared somber-faced at the black woman, the Asian, and the blonde Caucasian who'd dared to walk in.

Twyla said, "I didn't travel all the way from Maryland to get jumped."

There was fear in her eyes. There is never fear in Twyla's eyes. I waited a moment and wondered: Would we run out of there or eat our sought-after meat? I looked at Robin. Her eyes were more alive than I had ever seen them. She was smiling. The environment seemed to turn her on. She got us a waiter, and we sat down. The patrons continued to stare.

We looked like a microcosm of the United Nations on our way to Sunday school. Twyla named us "Salt, Pepper & Cayenne." We ordered freedom-loving ocean fish with heads still attached, and our nervous laughter soon turned joyous as the karaoke music got really, really good. Twyla and Robin started grooving to it, shimmying their shoulders as if they'd been born in this hood. We took pictures of our fish heads and devoured our hot plates of *frijoles autentico*. The man at the next table reached over and told us in broken English how happy he was that we were there. Then his wife offered me a beer. People continued to stare, only now, they were smiling. We were speaking charisma code, showing others, by learning their language, that we valued them. In response, this "foreign" land welcomed us and began to feel like home.

From the pages of this extraordinary work of love, passion, tears, joy, inspiration, sweat, and countless sleepless nights, if you remember nothing else, remember this: *"When you give people an experience of their Value, you live in their hearts forever."*

I will forever get to say that Robin and I met in the hallways of the Institute for Peace and Justice. It fits so well in the mythic story I am only just beginning to walk with her and *The Charisma Code*. Together, we are spinning a web of peace and justice to blanket the whole world. Peace and Justice is our revolution. As you learn to speak charisma code, you will create your own revolution, based on what matters the most to you. My wish for you, in Robin's words, is that you *let the desire to live as one of the Greats pump through your blood!*

When Robin thanked me for inviting her to launch *The Code* at the Annual Power of Collaboration event at the United Nations, a global summit I co-created with IMPACT's co-Founder, Constance J. Peak, my response to her was simple, "*The Charisma Code* is on a huge mission to drive change in how people value themselves and others. It needs an army to carry out this mission. As stubborn as I am, I'm also obedient, and I am honored to serve as one of your generals."

Yours in the journey of a beautiful Vita,
Janet C. Salazar
CEO and co-Founder, IMPACT Leadership 21
FSUN Permanent Representative to the United Nations

INTRODUCTION

At sixteen I left my American homeland for the continent of Africa. There I encountered the Kenyan culture, a culture completely alien from my Western upbringing. The food, dwellings, customs, and daily routines were all new. I didn't even speak the language, and yet, a magical thing happened: Instead of my feeling confused and alone, my interactions with the Kenyan people felt incredibly meaningful. Much more so than what I was accustomed to in my own country. I asked myself, "How is this possible? I can't even talk to them."

This question led me on a global adventure to discover what makes people feel connected to one another. I have lived in the most remote regions of Nepal, Sumatra, Sulawesi, Bali, Costa Rica, Guatemala, Spain, Thailand, Brazil, Mexico, and Nicaragua. Although traveling as an anthropologist, I was not trying to organize some grand display of human taxonomy. Instead, my travels have had one essential goal: to develop meaningful relationships without knowing the local languages. I wanted to understand *a language beyond words.*

So much communication flows from our bodies, betrays our upbringing, and advertises our personalities. I mimicked the ways different cultures swung their hips and kissed. I paid extra attention to how my body felt when passing individuals on the street. I sang with holy men and danced the local dances. I relied on a few staple sentences: "Hi," "Where's the bathroom?" and "Thank you."

With time, it occurred to me that there is already a word for what I was encountering: "charisma." Charisma is a universal language beyond words. It adds meaning to our words and our walk with gestures, vocal tone, and energy, delivering otherwise unarticulated information around our passion, our purpose, and how we value ourselves and the world. Charisma "speaks" to connect. Otherwise, why have it? What other purpose could charisma possibly serve than to establish connection?

During my travels, I wanted to open literal doors, step into foreign homes, and participate in local lifestyles, rituals, and the universalities of the human heart. And I did. Though I didn't know it at the time, I was using charisma to get *in*, and I learned a lot about culture.

Culture and charisma are closely linked: The people who are the best connectors are often the biggest influencers, and those who influence culture, change the world. Like charisma, culture speaks a language beyond words too. Culture invisibly transmits beliefs into your mind, like Wi-Fi talking to your smartphone. Culture is everything. It dictates whether we shoot the Big Bad Wolf in the woods or fall on our knees to praise his wildness. Culture tells you what to believe about yourself, informs the youth how to treat their elders, and governs how employees work together.

Culture is a democracy. We vote with our behavior, and cultures change quickly when one person communicates a behavior others deem valuable enough to want to copy. When you have charisma, others are likely to copy you. Charisma is both a personal and a cultural power.

On November 3, 2012 I went on all of my social media sites and posted the following picture of Bill Clinton, California Congressman Alan Lowenthal, and my mother.

In the caption I wrote:

> So my mom was telling me that being next to Clinton was like being plugged into an electrical socket. Where does that kind of charisma come from? What are his practices? . . . the practices of the Stars . . .

From that point forward I became a charisma detective on a quest for said "electrical socket." I wanted to find out where I— and anyone else willing and able to handle the current—could plug in, but try as I might, I could find no guide to cultivating this electromagnetic human charge. Did one exist?

In his article "Charm School," Mark Oppenheimer writes, "What's most striking about charisma studies is how few there are . . . . It's just seen as too elusive to waste one's time on."[1]

Waste one's time on?

For over two years I kept the company of my solitude, committed to making a shareable tool out of my rare life. I often writhed like a serpent in sand, searching for words and images that would hold relevance for you, my reader.

The result: this book.

In the final weeks of writing *The Charisma Code*, I was recruited to be president of a startup company called FreeCharging. Although I eventually declined the position, I learned quite a bit about alternative energy: by making electric-vehicle charging stations readily available, FreeCharging hopes to enable global sustainable transportation. By making charismatic principles readily available, *The Charisma Code* enables global *transformation*. Like electric vehicles, a charismatic person must plug in.

Question is: *Plug into what?*

People often associate charisma with a learned set of extroverted behaviors they must "put on" to be *wanted*. Nope. That is not how it works. The way you shake people's hands at a job interview will undoubtedly change after reading this material, but not because I told you how long you should hold their hand or what pressure to use.

True charisma comes from knowing you are safe, knowing you have something great to give, and knowing you can *connect* with anyone. The job of this book is to help your sinews realize this truth. When they do, your walk will change, your handshake will change, your emails will change, your life will change. You will stop hiding and start giving.

The first time I sent a book proposal for *The Charisma Code* to a traditional publishing house, the president sent me the following commentary—along with his rejection: "The author really thinks she's found the code for anyone to learn charisma? Tell her to go to Hawaii, Sedona, or Alaska and do a rewrite. She needs to tone it down a bit."

TONE IT DOWN? I don't think so, Mr. Publisher Man.

True charisma is gold, whether you are a business leader or an aspiring business leader; a safari guide or an aspiring safari guide; a playgirl or an aspiring playboy; an immigrant or a refugee; a prisoner or ex-offender. Charisma is gold for just about anyone or anything whose existence relies on connection. Charisma inspires engagement. It gets leads, motivates teams, and elicits commitment. It keeps the listener on the phone and eyes glued to what's next. It creates loyalty and rallies resolve. It opens doors, dissolves borders and makes any culture feel like home.

There is nothing "toned down" about my request. I am asking you, the reader, to plug in, charge up, and give your all! I am asking you to risk making *your best life*.

Welcome to *The Charisma Code*.

"F*** teaching them how to fish. Teach them how to commune with the fish."

JULIE WOODS, THE URBAN BLISS SHAMAN

CHARISMA
THE CURRENCY
OF CONNECTION

CHARISMA FACT
Not everyone is going to like you.

Face it: Who you are is a **bold** expression of life.
Escargot wrapped in pepperoni is not for everyone.

What you are about to read is not designed to be nice.
It is designed to call to your attention the importance
of being yourself.

CHARISMA: THE CURRENCY OF CONNECTION

Charisma's power stems from an inner confidence. This confidence magnetizes you, drawing people and opportunities irresistibly toward you. It creates the optimal environment for connection to occur. We are meant to be charismatic, to share the most authentic and valuable parts of ourselves; to communicate what Greek poet Evangelos Alexandreou called "the jewelry of the human soul." Unfortunately, like all coins, the Charisma Coin has a dark flipside . . .

FEAR: THE CURRENCY OF SEPARATION

The flipside of charisma is fear. Fear leads us to doubt we have anything valuable to share, convincing us our human gold is cheap brass. As a result, we resist opportunities to expose ourselves. The worst part is, when we deny the world our gifts, people and opportunities leave us, like animals fleeing a dry watering hole.

So what is charisma?

Charisma is a language beyond words. It "speaks" from the corners of eyes and tone of voice, position of foot and energy of handshake. Charisma helps communicate who you are. But charisma doesn't stop at your skin. It's a tool to bring others on your ride. Anyone can wield charisma. This book shows you how to harness the power of charisma so you can draw people together around a common goal, reveal gifts, and set souls on fire! Charisma is a choice. The choice between spending the currency of connection or spending the currency of separation. When you choose to spend the currency of connection, you *know your value, show your value,* and *see others' value.* When you choose to spend the currency of separation, you *forget your value, hide your value,* and *ignore others' value.* The latter choice says, "I can't risk putting myself out there. What if they don't like me or tell me I'm as unworthy as I secretly believe I am?" These thoughts hold you back from sharing your "soul's jewelry." You then vacate the premises before the premises can vacate you. Problem is, the premises will vacate anyway. You haven't left them anything to hang out with.

On the flip side, a person who has charisma is a person you want to spend time with. Someone whose hand you would fight to touch through a screaming crowd of fans. It's the quality that makes you want to date someone or vote them into office. The Beatles had it. Gandhi had it. Marilyn Monroe had it dripping off her eyelashes. It's what makes us feel connected to a person, even if we've never met them.

Nowadays, our pop-culture understanding of charisma is that it's an elusive, unnamable quality possessed by a handful of "special people." This belief is obvious on shows like *The X-Factor,* in which a panel of judges vote off most contestants because they don't measure up. Charisma is marketed as something either you have—or you don't. This belief is no accident. Charisma scarcity is manufactured by the entertainment business to make you value those "special people" more. It keeps a whole industry running, and it sells a lot of magazines.

But is charisma really a rare quality? Is it something that can only be possessed by a select few? I am here to tell you: it is not.

No matter what you grow up believing about yourself, you can cultivate charisma. In fact, you must. Finding your inner confidence is a necessary prerequisite to cultivating your magnetism, and magnetism is essential for making connections. Your ability to connect is the end-goal of this book, the key to getting laid and paid, and quite possibly the salvation of our planet. But just like building a bank account full of money, building a charisma currency account takes work. The work is not always easy, but it is simple, and I will guide you every step of the way. In the following chapters, I will walk you through charisma's three core constituents: confidence, magnetism, and connection. Prepare to be amazed. You have no idea what you are capable of.

STONE SOUP

Before we begin, you may ask, "Why is connection so important?"

Do you remember the story "Stone Soup"? It's an old fable about a village going through some pretty hard times. The starving villagers hoarded each bit of food for themselves, hiding alone behind closed doors. The people were secretive and suspicious, hungry and miserable.

One day, a stranger passing through town started a pot of boiling water in the town square. There was nothing in it but a stone. One curious villager asked him what he was making, and the stranger replied:

"Why, stone soup, of course! I'd be happy to share it with you, but it needs a parsnip."

The villager, who just happened to have a parsnip, exclaimed, "I've got a parsnip!" and ran home to get it. Then, one by one, each villager came to contribute one small thing to the pot: a potato, a carrot, a bit of salt, a dash of paprika. Before long, there was enough nourishing soup for the entire village. All it took was a little willingness to transform isolation and hoarding into collaboration and community.

After 3.8 billion years of evolutionary growth and pruning, nature is abundant with thriving, living systems. Nothing and nobody is wasted in the drive to survive. Every living thing is interconnected, contributing to the endurance and continuation of life on the planet. As UN Messenger of Peace Dr. Jane Goodall says, "Every individual matters and has a role to play in this life on earth."[1]

We tend to think of nature as "survival of the fittest," "red in tooth and claw." But it is also incredibly collaborative, with every being contributing in a vital way. As the Stone Soup fable illustrates, humanity is no exception. Our social nature requires us to make alliances with one another in order to survive. Some of us have carrots, and some have paprika. The point is, whatever you've got, we need it. Not convinced? Meet Dr. Tamsin Woolley-Barker.

Dr. Woolley-Barker is an evolutionary biologist. I met Tamsin in the jungles of Mexico. We bonded while trying to free a baby scorpion that had crawled into our tent. What were we doing way out there? We were studying nature, learning to mimic its 3.8 billion years of tried and true strategies for cool new inventions and ways of thinking. This process of mimicking nature's genius is called "biomimicry."

As Dr. Woolley-Barker explained to me, biomimics have figured out a basic rule of thumb concerning natural systems: nature supports systems that create conditions conducive to the flourishing of life.

It's as simple as that. Every cool adaptation in nature, be it flying squirrels or plants that eat bugs, has a role to play in our ecosystem. No trait exists in a vacuum. Every way of life creates opportunities (and problems) for the creatures around it. In fact, you can think of an organism's features less as "features" and more as nodes of interaction.

Of course, there are also animals that use what biologists call "cheater strategies." These species are commonly referred to as "parasites" and appear to take from their environment without giving back. But you know what? Parasites don't last long in large numbers. They have a high moment of glory, an explosion or a sprint, but over time, they (and their prey) must coadapt to a more harmonious equilibrium in order to survive. Think about it: if a parasite wipes out its free ride, it can kiss that way of life goodbye. Nature strikes a balance.

When I despair, I remember that all through history the
ways of truth and love have always won.
There have been tyrants, and murderers,
and for a time they can seem invincible,
but in the end they always fall.
Think of it—always.
MOHANDAS K. GANDHI

Our inquiry into parasites mixed with Gandhi makes for an appropriate cocktail to sip on during this early stage of our charisma exploration. The bitters provoke the question "Can charisma be used for hurt?" Why, yes, it can. *The Charisma Code* teaches you how to spark alive your charisma power. It does not, however, tell you what to do with the stuff once you're aglow. That part is up to you. So let's ask now, "What would you like to use your charisma power for?" As you consider the many ways, count on this: if charisma, like all of nature, is used to support the flourishing of life, it will last longer and ultimately outlive the charisma that's used to take from life.

The most successful species are those in which individuals work together and gift their abundance to one another. When we study these special creatures' survival strategies we find that, to them, gifting is synonymous with life.

So as members of this planetary party, we need each other. By the same logic, the world needs us. This is true of all species, but what about humans in particular? Oh boy, you guys and gals, it's about to get good!

THE SUPERORGANISM

You know ants? Of course you do. Well, the planetary biomass of ants is about the same as humans. That means if you rounded up all the ants that are alive right now, they would weigh about as much as all living human beings, and scientists estimate the worldwide population of termites may be *twenty-seven times higher than that*. What do termites and ants have in common? Along with a few other insects, they are extraordinary collaborators. The members of their colonies are so entwined, science has coined a term for them: "superorganisms."

A superorganism is a group of creatures so unified in purpose that they function as one.* Each individual plays a role in helping the superorganism function. For example, bees have a queen, the only one who gets to reproduce, while the soldiers and workers create a living situation favorable for the brood. Voilà! All these guys working together result in a superorganism called the hive. The hive wouldn't function if everybody did the exact same job. Imagine a thousand queens! Instead each individual acts out his or her innate gift. Thus, the hive thrives.

Guess who else is part of a superorganism? I'll give you a hint:

---

*The term "superorganism" is most often used to describe a *social unit* of *eusocial* animals, in which *division of labor* is highly specialized and individuals are not able to survive by themselves for extended periods of time. Eusociality is considered the most complex social structure in the animal kingdom, defined by the following characteristics: cooperative *brood* care (including brood care of offspring from other individuals), overlapping generations within a colony of adults, and a division of labor into reproductive and nonreproductive groups.

Our hunting-gathering groups acted
as one great forager,
scouring its range for a variety of food types,
a viable niche even in the midst of
professional carnivorous competitors like lions.

ANDREW WHITEN

Aw, yeah, you're sitting in one of their bodies. We humans are a superorganism too! This occurs very rarely outside insect colonies. Though Dr. Woolley-Barker suspects a few others (like some dolphins, including orcas), the only other mammal that we know for sure lives in a superorganism society is the naked mole rat. Once a year, the naked queen gives birth to as many as twenty-eight babies. She's the only one who gets to breed. The queen nurses her furless cuties for the first month, after which the other colony members feed them feces until they are old enough to forage for their own food. More than just feeding the babies these scrumptious feasts, these colony members collaborate to make sure the queen's kiddos are well groomed, accounted for, and kept warm. Naked mole rats are the longest living rodent (on average, thirty-one years) and do not get cancer. So basically, humans belong to a select group of incredible species that have evolved specifically to join forces with one another as a means of survival. Whoa.

Once you know this, it's kind of obvious. First of all, how in the world could humans' naked, furless, clawless bodies compete with the many furry, fangy, claw-clad beasts of the wild? I mean really, compared to a lion or jaguar, the human is a wimpy little ol' thing. I can hear you ask, "But what about fish? Don't fish cluster together in schools as a means of survival? Why aren't you calling that silver-bodied, singular direction a superorganism?" I'm glad I heard you ask about the fish, as this marks an important distinction: schools of fish are not superorganisms, because their roles are all interchangeable. A superorganism species requires its members to each contribute his or her unique, specialized gift, or shall we say, a superorganism species requires its members to each contribute his or her special spice to the stew.

Conclusion: Our species' overwhelming success means there are other survival strategies at work. The fact that we're a superorganism species is one of the biggies. We see modern examples of our superorganism finesse in team sports, government, and putting on a play. Also, every corporation exists because of its ability to work as a superorganism. Seeing a company act as one body through its aligned purpose and vision is nothing short of thrilling. The corporate environment is one of my primary venues for teaching the principles in *The Charisma Code*. One of the strongest factors I use to predict a company's long-term success or demise is whether or not its employees work as a collaborative superorganism, a necessary skill for an organization whose name, "corporation," can be defined as "a group of people acting as one body."

The way we take care of one another also shows our superorganism nature. Did you know that dolphins are the only species with menopausal females besides us? This is biologically significant. In nature, life forms die quickly once they are no longer reproductive. But in the case of humans and certain types of dolphins, nature considers the grandmas valuable enough to stick around. The reason? When we're done making babies, we still support conditions conducive to life. We provide care for our babies' babies (dolphin grandmothers even lactate!), care for other members of our community, and the gift of wisdom from a life well lived. Superorganism in effect! When we're not blinded by our obsession with youth and fertility, biology shows us that elders are a necessary part of a functioning human superorganism. If this were not true, the females would die after menopause.

If you live in a fast-paced, advertisement-encrusted, dog-eat-dog kind of reality, it may be hard to see humanity's superorganism potential, but I promise you that under less stressful conditions, this life-conducive practice is thriving. Here's an example: I was sixteen, on a bus in Kenya, watching a man with his baby in one arm and groceries in the other. It was obviously hard to hold his bag and his priceless, cooing cargo. Riding on a standing-room-only bus, he had nowhere to put down his groceries. To my amazement, I watched as he handed his baby to a complete stranger. There were no words exchanged, just smiles. When that passenger got off, he just handed the man's baby to someone else. Again, when that man got off the bus, he handed the baby to yet another stranger. A baby needed to be held, and for a little while, her father couldn't do the holding. There were no questions asked, no "Please" or "This is why." Just an unspoken availability to be of use to another human.

There is one essential ingredient that allowed the scene above to play out: Trust. All high-functioning superorganism societies require it. I need you to perform your function for *my* survival, and you need me to perform my function for *yours*. When we share the same goal, we trust our "teammates" to do everything they can to make it happen. Their success is our success. If we choose not to cooperate, we lose our hive or it gets sick. Everyone must contribute or everyone suffers.

Have you ever been stranded on the side of the road and had someone pull over to ask if you're okay? Next thing you feel are tears welling up because you are so touched that this perfect stranger is caring for you? It's why Jack Canfield's book series, *Chicken Soup for the Soul,* is such a smashing success. It reminds us, in its own words, that we are part of a superorganism. Humans are deeply interlocked and interwoven. What we do to ourselves, we do to one another. Although we often get confused about who we are, the way we feel when we are cared for by a stranger quickly reminds us.

The way our superorganism society works, we can't even turn on a light without hundreds or thousands of others, each one playing a crucial role: manufacture the bulb, package it, ship it, ring it up at the counter, wire our homes for electricity, run the power plant, et cetera. All this to bring us light. Think about that the next time you flip a switch.

Bottom line, on a purely evolutionary level, humans are designed to connect. Without connection, there's no light, no team, no soup. You are part of this tasty broth, and no one in the world is quite the vegetable that you are. You must gift your gifts!

While giving often seems counterproductive in the short term, it is productive in the long term. Relationships take time to develop enough to provide value we can see. Rest assured, each time you act as a giver, you are also giving to yourself. In his book *Give and Take*, Wharton professor Adam Grant explains how "givers" (those who help others without selfish motivation), "takers" (those who take without giving in return), and "matchers" (those who strive for equal trades) can affect our success— both as individuals and at the corporate level. Here's one tidbit: Evidence suggests that in sales, givers begin with 6 percent lower revenue than takers and matchers. But by the year's end, givers finish with a gargantuan 68 percent higher revenue![2]

WHAT IF . . . ?

So we, some bugs, and those cool naked mole rats share this superorganism thing, but do we humans have anything that is unique to us? You know, the anteater is best at eating ants, the cactus is best at living in the desert. What are we best at? What is our "superpower?"

Some say that humans are separate from nature. This is simply not true. Look around you. Everything you see is part of nature. This includes plastic Barbies and Budweiser caps, which, however processed or far removed from the source, did in fact come from nature: just like us! But there is something else unique about us. As Dr. Woolley-Barker puts it, "We influence our evolution more than any other species by asking, 'What if . . . ?'"

That's right. You don't see ants practicing biomimicry. Only humans do that. Why? The answer is quite specific. Humans have a genetic basis for understanding time in a sequential, narrative way. We tell stories. As storytellers we choose what we want to create and grow into. We time-travel in our minds. When we ask, "What if . . . ?" we're imagining how things might be different in an alternate reality. You know, different from right now. Religion, inventions, stories, promises: these things all come from the ability to imagine parallel realities. Our species' ability to ask "What if . . . ?" opens us to an infinity of choice. It is this question-asking ability that allows us to influence our evolution.

What if . . . I cut my hair?
What if . . . I could end world hunger?
What if . . . I could get out of debt?
What if . . . I could be happier?
What if . . . there's a better way?
What if. . . I could get charisma?
What if . . . I could climb the castle wall like a gecko?

I like to think "whatiferousness" is our superpower, the magic wand into infinite possibility. Unfortunately, it often hurts us as well, by keeping us constantly going around in "what if" circles.

What if . . . I'm late?
What if . . . they don't like me?
What if . . . I make a mistake?

We spend a lot of time using "What if?" to cultivate fear. It's not difficult to see that humans, as a species, are suffering as a result. Even first-world countries (mostly them!) register sky-high levels of depression. Author Brendon Burchard points directly to this epidemic in his book *The Charge*. "Face it: the emotional energy of the world has flatlined. Over the past forty years, across almost every developed country in the world, the diagnosis of clinical depression has grown nearly tenfold."[3] Like the superhero burned before he learns to master his superpower, so it is with our mental time machine. As long as we use our power for fear and separation instead of love and connection, we will suffer. We must choose our questions with care. As soon as you ask a question, your mind starts grinding away to crank out an answer. You can't help it; it's what your human brain is made to do. But you can fabricate a lasso for that magnificent mind of yours and reel it in when you notice your question-asking cycles teetering on the edge of destruction.

How? Stop asking questions that hurt! Critical thinking and debate can be illuminating. I am not suggesting you stop asking the hard questions of yourself and others. I am, however, suggesting you stop asking the questions that encourage verbal self-flagellation. If you've been asking "what-if-I-f—ed up" type questions for a good portion of your life, putting down the whip may be harder than you think. We will explore this process more deeply in the next chapter. But go ahead and start using your whatiferousness superpower for love and connection right now by asking the question "What if I never feel the urge to ask another belittling question again?"

Let's garner a better idea of how your whatiferousness works by taking a look at the question, "What if I could climb the castle wall like a gecko?"

Think about it for a minute. Ask yourself, "What if I could climb the castle wall like a gecko?"

Notice how your brain immediately starts wondering how the gecko climbs walls.

Are his feet sticky? Are they webbed? Could I create a pair of wall-climbing shoes that mimic the gecko's castle-climbing capabilities?

The fancy word for this mimic-creation process is "reverse-engineering." Whatever you put your human imagination to, your mind automatically tries to make so. Granted, climbing castle walls might not be number one on your bucket list, but I bet there are other things you would like to use your blood-pumping, full-breathed creative juices for. Maybe you want to solve the California drought. Maybe you want to date Paris Hilton. Maybe you want to learn how to get the spot out of your carpet. Your brain can't tell the difference. They're all questions to be considered, imagined, and turned into results. The mental magic starts with a question, and you get to pick which ones you ask.

As Jesus Christ, one of the first people in history to be called a "charismatic" leader[4] said, "Ask and you shall receive."[5]

Here's the deal: Humans would not possess the ability to ask "What if?" unless it supported conditions conducive to life. Further, humans evolved to function as superorganisms, so whatiferousness must be a condition conducive to life. Riddle me this, Grasshopper: If only some of us were meant to manifest change, to influence our species; if only some of us were meant to create life-enhancing conditions; if only some of us were supposed to be charismatic rebels, how come we can all ask, "What if?"

WRAPPIN' IT UP

Why is connection so important? Because our species literally needs your gifts to survive.

In addition to the survival component, connection is a prerequisite for safety, a necessity for collaboration, a cure for apathy, and a lubricant for joy. Trust me, you want it.

The next three chapters will guide you through the cultivation and spending of your charisma currency. I will share with you exercises to help build new patterns in your daily life, working towards the goal of connecting authentically with others.

Here's a sneak preview into one of the ways it all works; charisma's three powers will often interplay like this:

1. When you activate your *confidence* by knowing your value,
2. You show up to life in a way that *magnetizes* others to you, and
3. Once people are magnetized to you, you are in a prime position to use *The Charisma Code*'s global communication tools to establish powerful *connection*.

Charisma does not dictate what you will do with connection once you have it. You and the person with whom you are connecting decide that. Charisma simply opens the door for the connection to occur.

Once you are abundant with charismatic currency, *The Charisma Code* will show you how to spend it in the way that best serves your unique gifts and desires. Whether you are looking to get laid, paid, or start a revolution; whether you are more like Marilyn Monroe, the Dalai Lama, Einstein, Oprah, or Martin Luther King Jr. (you are more like one of them than you know!); you will be replete with charisma currency, and it will burn a hole in your pocket until you spend it well!

Charisma spending takes a little effort on your part, but once you get the hang of it, I guarantee you will find it challenging to stop. Each time you spend a little, you will infect someone else, and making someone or something light up is habit-forming.

This final step of *The Charisma Code* is rarely taught in charisma manuals or charm schools. It's the real deal.

Let's face it: Being attractive and refined is not really what you're after. What you want is what comes from attracting engagement: the possibility of true love, a promotion, or, if you're the Ché Guevara type, revolution. You will achieve none of the above if you attract but do not connect. To remedy that missed opportunity, let us see you, listen to you, love you, worship you, orbit around you. Then, when you're ready, turn the tables a full 180 degrees and see us.

However, know this: the Charisma Coin is round for a reason. You can start by developing what this manual calls "Step One, Confidence: *Know Your Value*" or you can start by developing "Step Three, Connection: *See Others' Value*." Although it's comforting to imagine you can follow three steps in order and 1 + 1 will equal 2, as you read *The Charisma Code* you will discover that more often, 1 + 1 equals 3. Logic is comforting but logic is rarely all there is.

Charismatic currency will rush into your bank account when you employ all three steps simultaneously. For some of you, the three steps to charisma will ignite into a burst of singularity when you start by activating charisma's electric mixture with "Step One, Confidence: *Know Your Value.*" While for others of you, the spark will emit from your eyes when you begin developing your charisma by focusing on "Step Three, Connection: *See Others' Value.*"

My suggestion: read this baby through and let it sink into your sinews. Then go out in the world and practice following your own lead with regards to which part of the Code to implement in any given circumstance. For many of us, knowing our value is the most heroic challenge we face. If that's you, you can take the back door to confidence by training yourself to see others' fabulousness first.

Don't want to wait to finish this book before activating your charisma code? You're my kind of *Homo sapiens*! The following figure goes out to you. It outlines a charisma hygiene practice that, as your charismologist, I recommend you perform daily—if not hourly. Follow the arrows like you are following the golden-brick road—you will not be disappointed.

CHARISMA HYGIENE

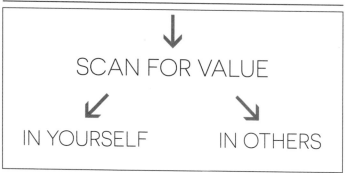

STEP ONE
CONFIDENCE
Know Your Value

CHARISMA RULE
Know you are made of great stuff.

We cannot fight war with war, but we can entice war to lay down its guns. Charisma disarms with charm.

As a little girl, I remember disarming my grouchy, old, sick grandpa, my Popo, with hula dances and surprise hugs. I put gel in his bangs till they stood tall like 1980s *Cosmopolitan* models. Then we'd go to the mirror and laugh together. He barked this or that and I just giggled. I knew he loved me.

Because I was one of the few who didn't get offended by the armed grouch in him, he enjoyed being with me. He gave me stuffed animals and "ahhrng juice" (what any genuine East Coaster calls their breakfast beverage).

Before my Popo died, he took me to the collection of medals he'd earned in World War II as a bombardier. He opened their glass case and told me to take good care of them after he passed. Oh, my Popo knew how to fight all right. As a New York orphan, he also knew how to survive.

I loved making my Popo happy. And I think he loved me most because he loved who he was when he was with me. Not the fighter. Not the survivor. Just the grandpa whose granddaughter giggled when he got grouchy. That is how charisma disarms. Its grace forgives curmudgeons their lack of grace, and suddenly, they find it.

I was twelve years old when my Popo died. When I got the call, I ran outside to the top of the big, wild hill behind my house, threw off my clothes, and played my blue ocarina clay flute. I knew only one song, and I played it over and over again. In my own rain, sun rays through cloud, wind on my skin, I played this song to him:

"Amazing Grace,
how sweet the sound,
That saved a wretch
like me.
I once was lost
but now am found,
Was blind,
but now I see."

JOHN NEWTON

1. THE GIFT OF GRACE

[S]uddenly, a light from heaven flashed about him. And he fell to the ground and heard a voice saying to him, 'Saul, Saul, why do you persecute me?' . . . Saul arose from the ground; and when his eyes were opened, he could see nothing. And for three days he was without sight, and neither ate nor drank. (Acts 9: 3-9)

After this experience, Saul became known as Paul. His three days of blindness and fasting were extremely somatic and must have been physically trying, yet he recounts them as a mystical experience with God. So much so that Paul went on to write about this event in the epistles, describing it as "a gift of God's grace."[1]

How could such a clearly traumatic event have been experienced as a gift of grace? That's where it gets interesting, because while describing this gift from on high, Paul coined a word: "charisma." The word itself is a combination of *charis*, which historians believe was the Greek colloquial for the word "grace-gift," and *-ma*, the Greek suffix for "act of."

The concept was twofold: when one received an act of grace (charis-ma) from God, one would keep one's gift alive by giving it! For example, let's say someone is endowed with the gift of inspiring others with their words. Whenever they open their mouth, they are spreading their divine gift of gab. Charisma is a gift that keeps on giving, like a snowball or an economic stimulus package. It was never meant to be an attribute, as much as a force, a currency. Like any currency, charisma moves through the community. And, like currency, charisma has to come from somewhere before it can circulate. Money originates at the governmental Bureau of Engraving and Printing. Charisma comes from a divine source to a grounded recipient. From that recipient, it can radiate to the community. You too can be an unending well of value for your global community, but, like Paul, in order to give your gift, you must first receive it.

In this chapter, we will discover how to receive your grace-gift directly, by becoming still and allowing the "lightning from on high" to strike. As success coach and empowerment giant Tony Robbins says, "Passion wakes you up to something in life that you desire so strongly that you no longer have to push yourself to do anything. You now have a different kind of drive; a force that *pulls* you forward."[2] Once that fire is lit within you, you glow with the passion of knowing you have something to give. That knowing will give you confidence, and confidence, young Grasshopper, is the first step in your charisma training.

AUTHOR'S NOTE

There is no clear consensus on the nature of God.

WIKIPEDIA "GOD" PAGE

Can I talk about "God" for a sec? A three-letter word that has brought undeniable peace, joy, and sanity for many, while on the flip-side it has been a vehicle for our collective *insanity* through holy wars, child molestation cover-ups, and outright scams.

Why do I need to talk about God at all? I mean, I'm here to teach you how to unlock your charisma code, right? The thing is, the more I delve into decoding charisma, the more I encounter countless surprises, all of them pointing towards the mysterious, the ineffable, *language beyond words*. There has to be something responsible for all of *this*, right? I love science, but people, I need to know one thing: What *banged* the big bang?

When I began research for this book, the fact that the word "charisma" had its coming-out party in the Bible was news to me. Raised a Jewish Pagan who celebrated Christmas, I was initially exposed to the Bible in hotel rooms. Because of my previously limited exposure, I feel I've had the opportunity to explore Christianity from a perspective of innocence and discovery. I hope you will join me in that innocence as we visit charisma's roots.

THE IMMEDIATE CONTEXT

First off, we should talk about why you're not crazy confident in the first place. This is a serious question. It's safe to assume that, soon after conception, we are all confident, because we . . . *are*. We exist. Against all odds, we've got a heartbeat and trillions of cells just for us. We land in the womb with no reason to believe we are anything less than life's favorite bambino. That being the case, it should be easy to sit still, look inside, and immediately get high on the glory of existing, but, for most of us, it's not that easy. Somewhere along the way, we lost our sense of worth. Why? you may ask. Well, there are a couple of reasons. Let's take a look at them. And then we'll smash on through to confident badassery.

Let's start by examining your immediate circumstances. If you reside in the West, you're in a hypercommercialized society, bombarded with constant advertising. Traditional advertising works by making you dissatisfied with what you have and who you are. It's pretty simple: in order to get you to buy something, the seller must convince you that you'd be happier if you did so. But what if you are already happy? Bad news for the seller, that's what.

This is why, when you watch a commercial for a product, often the first thing they want you to know is that you're lacking, and you should be dissatisfied about it. In the next moment, they offer a solution: here's our product to save the day! Next time you see a commercial, pay attention. You'll see it everywhere. It's the same reason that impossible standards of wealth and beauty are modeled on, oh, you know, billboards and pamphlets and bus benches and TV screens and the side of your Facebook page. We are constantly shown a mirage of social perfection beyond the horizon, forever out of reach. A carrot dangling before the bridle. Thought you had the best phone? Nope, there's a new one. Can't keep up? Don't worry. We can help with that.

Truth is, these advertisements are speaking to our actual pain, our fear of becoming an irrelevant, insignificant, lackluster, disposable commodity. These advertisements work only when we believe we are incomplete. These advertisements work only when we flaccidly allow ourselves to ask, "What if I am incomplete?" The question becomes, "Who made up this fear, them or us?"

THE HISTORICAL CONTEXT

Ever since Adam took the bait and bit right into that scrumptious Red Delicious, Western humans have lived with two powerful but dangerous ideas:

1. We know right from wrong; and
2. We are not only capable of sin, but bound to commit it. It's in our very nature. You could even say it's part of our job description.

Organized religion has used these concepts to manipulate millions ever since, offering direction on how to stay on the "right side" of God's good grace. While there is nothing inherently "wrong" with religious guidance, in the tenth and eleventh centuries CE, we took the external-judgment train a bit too far and ended up at the end of the line: the Dark Ages, a time of extreme control and punishment.

Then, 700 years ago, Western people enjoyed a fun explosion of art and culture. During the Renaissance, a time of spiritual refreshment, joy and new ideas blossomed like lilies in the field. But this too has passed, and all that merrymaking transitioned into the "Age of Disenchantment," when the lilies were machine-mowed down and replaced by an Astroturf of rational, visible, fact-based reality. A new and powerful addiction to the quantifiable wrapped its know-it-all tongue into the gaping holes of our holiness. It declared ownership of the unknown. It called the enchanted gardens and beliefs of animist villagers "primitive" and "ignorant," and it has been raising its scrupulous head ever since.

The result? We now live in a culture that values the rational over the romantic. But even our best scientists, while excellent at measuring the very small and the very big, still cannot measure the Infinite. We can measure the big bang, but who banged it?

There is a big, embarrassing hole in our cultural logic, which states that all things can be explained, and if they cannot, they are silly (as if there's something wrong with silly). Rational is more adult, and so, more credible. Intuition, wonder, and awe are fairytales, things we grow out of when we are mature. Right? Nay, nay, my friend. Listen up to Albert Einstein: "And certainly we should take care not to make the intellect our god; it has, of course, powerful muscles, but no personality. It cannot lead, it can only serve; and it is not fastidious in its choices of a leader."[3]

Despite our factual society, not one of us *Homo sapiens* was born this way. We arrived innately enchanted with the untamable wonders of life! Swayed by its wet, diamond-tipped leaves and sometimes-warm, sometimes-cold winds, we loved being surprise-kissed by the waves meeting the seashore. We laughed and squealed. Nature programmed us that way. We are born scientists, designed to explore, to play, to wonder, *What if . . . ?* Remember?

PLAY?

The field of play science is expanding. Scientists like Stuart L. Brown from the National Institute for Play in Carmel Valley, California, suggest that play is not just fun, it is tied to our survival as a species. Dr. Brown tells us that, just as asking "what if?" is an integral part of our human survival strategy as a super-organism, so too is play a part of what keeps our species highly adaptive. But here's the rub: in one generation alone, childhood playtime outside has decreased by 71 percent in both the United States and the United Kingdom. Seventy-one percent! Ouch. Dr. Brown writes, "At the far end of serious major play deprivation, a review of the mass murderers who have either been grievance killers, or potentially those with a psychotic core, has, in the majority, demonstrated that healthy play was seriously missing in their lives."[4] Okay. This is a warning to modern-day Westerners to bring back the wildness of childhood in which open lots breed rough and tumble play and other children-organized explorations of their world. But now I need to talk to you about your life.

Although Western culture shames citizens who aren't busily working away the tick-tock of their day, the resulting symptoms of adult play-deprivation are anything but charismatic. Here's what Dr. Brown found as the byproducts of adults withholding play from their daily lives: lack of vital life engagement; diminished optimism; stuck-in-a-rut feeling about life, with little curiosity or exploratory imagination to alter their situation; predilection to escapist temporary fixes such as alcohol (or other compulsions); a personal sense of being life's victim rather than life's conqueror. In sum: withholding play from your life is NOT what you should do if you're looking to increase your charisma quotient.

THE ANSWER

Back to the question at hand: Why aren't we confident? We are born full of wonder and reverence for Reality, in all its splendor and mystery, but culture condemns us for being "childish," "naive," and "uneducated." A gaping hole exists in our souls, a hunger to be exploited by advertisers offering comfort-stuffed Band-Aids: food, fashion, cigarettes, cinema, boobs, botox, and booze. The only reason this works is because a poisonous seed was planted long, long ago. This one old, stupid idea that keeps people scared, makes us behave, and threatens us with hellfire. You ready? I hinted at it before. Here it is:

GREAT STUFF VERSUS BAD STUFF

That's it. It came with our apple-eating, Garden of Eden, cultural mythology. While you may have placed your attention on the main point (God's wrath at the biblical couple's newfound ability to tell right from wrong), you may have missed the underlying message: that "good" and "bad" exist at all. See, when we feel bad about ourselves, there's something really subtle going on, but it only seems subtle because it's been hammered into us, over hundreds of years, to the point that we barely think to question it.

The ideas of good and evil are deeply ingrained in our cultural mythology, but when we use these dichotomies for any reason whatsoever, we apply a dangerous logic: If some characters are worthy of love and others are not, if some cleaning supplies are evil and others are our friends, if some clothes are so last season and others are fabulous, if some countries are terrorist nations and others are our buddies—do you see the pattern? Whether we're talking about people, products, pants, or politics—we've been told that matter can be made of *bad stuff*.

We've lost touch with the greatness in *all* things. We think that maybe only *some* of the matter on earth is good and we should be frantically collecting that stuff and discarding the bad. Since we're taught that we can't trust ourselves to know which is which, we learn to fear what we have and reach for the next thing. If you aren't carrying the latest touchpad device, advancing your career, or fixing your body flaws, then maybe you are not good enough. Maybe *you* are the bad stuff. Somebody is. It could be you!

This fear of inadequacy paralyzes us. When you feel the guilt that comes with thinking you are bad stuff, your body releases inflammatory substances. Inflammation is what we find when there is trauma to or infection in the body's tissues. Here's the kicker: You make it yourself. Your guilt and shame send a signal to your body, telling you that you're being attacked. In response, your body sends floods of fluids and fighter cells to protect itself. In other words, the state of guilt and shame is a physical attack.

You're fighting yourself. Your body cannot tell the difference between your thoughts and a virus. The resulting inflammation is systemic and leads to all kinds of nastiness.

Tragically, in this lush first world of ours, many people spend their whole lives fighting the bad feelings the only way they know how: by earning small change to purchase short-term self-medication in the aforementioned forms of food, fashion, cigarettes, cinema, booze, boobs, and erectile-tissue enhancers. The result? In the United States, the richest nation on earth, depression is epidemic.

Here's the good news: None of that logic works on you if you stop believing in bad stuff. When you choose to believe you're made of great stuff, you have no need to waste your time being afraid and insecure, so your body has no need to send unnecessary inflammatory fighter responses, and you can get back to the good sh——t: exploring yourself, exploring your environment, and getting in touch with *this f——ing moment!* Are you ready to stop asking what if I'm not enough and start asking what if I am? If you're okay with being a cultural rebel, sincerely ask yourself the following question right now: What if I am enough?

You are. The rest is makeup. Grace is the state we are in when we are doing nothing but just being who we are.

Next question is: Are you ready to stop running and start experiencing? I warn you: The charge of the here and now is electrifying! Rasping and riveting, laughing and belly hurting, tingling and cringing, smashing and contracting, expanding and orgasming. It's messy and it's wet and it bubbles over sometimes. There is phlegm. Oh, yeah. Living in the present demands every fiber of your being, and it will force you to grow and blossom and vomit out magic in ways you never thought possible; and you've been trained to run away from it your whole life. But baby, I'm here to tell you, it's what you were born for. Are you ready to choose it? It's not going to be easy. It's going to be great!

"In the beginning was the Word. (John 1:1) Before the Word was . . . THE."

THE-: [COMBINING FORM. FROM GREEK THEOS: GOD]

THE CHOICE

I believe that God is our highest
instinct to know ourselves.

DEEPAK CHOPRA

One night, I was unable to sleep. Anxious thoughts riddled my mind, and I struggled to calm myself. Eventually I got up to stand by the window, and by chance, I found myself admiring the curve of my shoulder under my nightgown. Then I looked up to the perfectly green ivy growing on the Los Angeles stucco, and I felt the caress of the cool air between us. That's when it dawned on me, as it sometimes does, that I have absolutely no idea where this life came from.

I imagined the magnificent pictures taken by NASA showing spirals upon spirals of galaxies above me and felt the impending squish from this uncontrollably large universe, like an ant under a human foot en route to Starbucks, and you know what? I liked it. It made me more present, like a hot needle pressing skin. Here I Am! In the midst of eternity, I exist! Next time you think you or your circumstances suck, go outside and look up. In the presence of the vast, wordless sky, you'll see those negative thoughts are really all just little stuff. But we often forget. And when we do, confidence gets lost.

The key to feeling confident in the middle of a wildly distracting world is perspective, and the only way to gain any real perspective is by anchoring yourself firmly in the present. How can you know how to relate to what is around you unless you know who, what, and where you are? There are simple tools to get you there . . . or here, as the case may be. Let's start at the beginning.

Have you ever noticed that when you pause to take a deep breath or become attentive to your lover's breath, a sense of peace washes over you? Maybe you've felt peaceful when you are deeply engaged in making music or writing a poem? How about when you look at the colors in a sea-blown sunset or smell the clarity in mountain air? Maybe you experience peace most when you're racing cars or rock climbing? When do you recall a time when you felt truly at peace?

Peace comes when we are fully engaged with whatever we are doing. Another name for this is *presence*. The more you spend time engaged with the present, the more people will experience you as "larger than life," "a charismatic personality," someone they themselves want to engage with. Being engaged with the present means you have chosen to be curious with where you are, what's around you, and how you're feeling. When you're present, you're open and porous to experience and ready to let it have its way with you. It's really rather sexy. Plus you'll no longer have a need to be exploited by advertisers when gallivanting in a field of crickets or when quietly knitting a quilt becomes exhilarating for you. All the present asks for before it will fill you with its vitality-enhancing sanity is that you put down your defenses, abstractions, and even your what ifs so it can . . . um . . . enter you.

Note: In many parts of the world, people, often called monks, dedicate their entire lives to figuring out how to spend as many moments as possible becoming one with the present. Do you know what these monks are really doing, though? In charisma code speak, they are learning how to master their whatiferousness. They are learning how to leave their questioning minds so that an even higher intelligence, believed to exist in every now, can impregnate them with a wholeness and an insight so great, they remember who they are. This is what I call "THE." In the beginning was the Word, but before the Word itself, is "THE." "THE" is a prefix to all things. The Word doesn't exist until you have THE. Nothing exists until you have THE.

How does THE relate to charisma? It has to do with the confidence that comes from knowing who you are. Whatever you think you are, you're not. You're more. THE is a way of remembering that there is a mysteriously massive and impeccably clean slate available to you in every moment. You're not stuck in what you think you are. You're not stuck in the words other people use to describe you either. You are vast like space itself. You are made of a language beyond words. Baby, you were born with charisma!

Just as words are symbols, so are your thoughts. They are mere clouds floating through your mental sky. You make them up. Sometimes you think thoughts that empower you, while other times you think thoughts that usurp your power. We all do it, right? The question remains, to which thoughts do you give attention?

One common energy drain is to leave the present moment and go gallivanting about in the future. Perhaps you can relate. Has your mind ever strayed from your work, thinking about what to eat for lunch? Then, when you're eating lunch, do you find yourself thinking about what's next at work? Get back in your body! The difference between thinking about eating your sandwich and actually eating it is the difference between reading a menu and crunching that hot aioli toast between your teeth.

Likewise, the past clamors for your attention. Have you ever been hung up on a conversation you wish had gone differently, a mistake you think you made, or a lost relationship you now imagine was perfect? The past is so much less energized than the present. When you live in the past, you become a shadow of yourself. In order to cultivate charismatic currency, you have to stay current. Exchange all of those little-stuff thoughts swimming around in your cranium, the ones based in the past or the future, and embrace the big stuff. Love, joy, and passion live in the present, so let's get your mind back to this succulent moment. This will require focus.

You can't make fire with a magnifying glass if your hand is wiggling around. You need a steady, still hand to gather the sun and start the fire. Using this analogy, I like to think of the sun as a life force available to us in any given moment, if we stop and sip the stillness. Out of this stillness comes novel ideas.

Out of this stillness comes life, and out of this stillness comes fiery passion. Any moment our minds stop playing ping pong, a huge rush of energy floods into our bodies. Still thoughts are like the steady magnifying glass, focusing life force into fire, into creation. Creativity, inspiration, and innovation are born here. *In this creative crucible, it is obvious we are made of great stuff,* and when you realize you are made of great stuff, you rip off the mask that occludes your confidence.

As mentioned, we Western folk are trained to be on the run from immediate circumstance. When you first attempt to stay present, you may encounter resistance personalities like these:

- THE WORRY WART: With the slightest tinge of fear, our instinctual brain looks for a handhold of safety. I might forget to pick my daughter up from school . . . . I better keep thinking about it, so I don't "lose myself in the moment" and forget.

- THE SHRINKING COCK: If there is a strong sensation or emotion we don't know how to deal with, we find a way to bypass the uncomfortable, unknown, and over-whelmingly powerful sensations by retreating to our dismal, calculating, video-game mind, trying to predict every possible outcome and plan every inch before-hand. Bo . . . ring.

- THE BELIEVER: The same way an apple falling from a tree picks up speed as it falls, so your thoughts gain momentum the longer you believe them. The believer is compelled to trust the mind's fantastical imaginings as gospel. Usually, the believer is one who feels one's thoughts strongly. Your body responds to worry, doubt, and desire so intensely that it is challenging to just stop spinning that mental hamster wheel. I must find a solution! This is real! There is a problem! The problem is, the more you look at the problem, the more of a problem it becomes. The believer has a way out, though; it is the same savior we all have, the ever-present, neutral, soft and expansive, deeply intelligent, and trustworthy present. All the believer needs to do is deem these thoughts unworthy of their time. One more time: All the believer needs to do is deem these thoughts unworthy of their time. This sets the believers free to believe a new story; the one happening *right now*. (Note: If you try to stop your mental hamster wheel via command but continue to spin back onto the wheel, best you go do something physical.)

These knee-jerk reactions to being present may be discouraging, but like any habit, we can make it stick with repetition and conviction. Make a valiant choice to bring yourself back to the vibrant aliveness in each sensory moment. Remember: Only you can turn the knob on how much life you let inhabit every second. The present, by its very nature, can never leave you. It does not matter how frightened, confused, or angst-ridden you feel, the present is "the gift of grace" that every charismatic learns to stretch out in.

Want to turn your faucet knob full throttle with the pomegranate juice of now? Take a hint from the ancient Masters and do the simplest thing in the world: Sit still, watch your breath, and don't be afraid of what you feel.

2. THE BRAIN

Ask yourself: *Is my behavior getting me the results I want?*

I asked a cognitive neuroscientist friend of mine, Dr. Andrew Hill, what the function of our brain is. He told me the brain is "a pattern-matching machine. Its job is to maximize benefit and reduce risk, by identifying patterns from previous experience in incoming information." That great wiry, curlicued electric miracle of your brain serves one function: it makes patterns!

Think about it: Patterns are necessary for survival. Recognizing bright orange spherical things on the edges of tree branches can keep you alive. The more we think or do something, the more our brains assign relevance to it. "Oh," says the brain, "she's done that a lot; it must be important. I will keep my eye out for it and be ready to respond the way she's practiced (fight it, love it, or ignore it)."

Bless our brain's pattern-making ability. It is greatly responsible for why we are the most adaptable species on earth, but we can also create some pretty nasty unintentional patterns. Patterns are like ruts, wagon-wheel pathways our brain runs over and over because we keep practicing them. Sometimes we practice the wrong thing, and then it's hard to get out of those well-worn, mud-hardened grooves. Our biology is efficient; it won't go out of its way to change a patterned route. Nope. If left to its own devices, the brain will keep on running the pattern that you (and your parents and your culture) have had you practicing since birth. Same old self-deprecating thoughts. Same old late-night cake and cookie dough, same old running away before "maybe...."; same old little tiny, insignificant, grey-walled thought loops—on and on and on and on and on and on and on—and they suck. They suck the life out of your would-be larger-than-life charisma. Misidentifying these rut-thoughts as a dictation of who we are tethers us, like a warm tongue on the frigid metal of a frozen winter flagpole. Helpless, hurting, humiliated, we have only courage enough to howl in silence.

But all is not lost. You have the power to completely repattern your brain routes. You're the driver. You can take the wheel of your brain and drive it on a new pathway. A route nobody has seen before.

What is this power? Why, it's you! Neuroscientists say it takes between three to five weeks of repeating a pattern to form a new habit. The more you practice, the more that pattern becomes your new go-to, knee-jerk response. Not only do your existing cells (with millions of interconnections) remap when you learn new things, but you also add new cells. In just three to five short weeks, those little synapse coyote trails become the new wagon trail to glory.

Three to five weeks. That means be patient with yourself. Don't give up. It won't be easy; you're fighting to get out of ruts built over a lifetime. Like toboggan tracks in snow, the longer you've careened down that path, the deeper the grooves. Without active perseverance and determination, the old behaviors your parents, teachers, culture, and everything you ever thought about yourself—positive or negative, true or false—will do their damnedest to keep you rolling in those ruts. Is that what you want? Of course not! Remember to ask yourself, "Is my behavior getting me the results I want?" If not, you can change it, a little at a time, but consistently over time. Nothing succeeds like success, and overcoming challenges is what makes success so rich. When we do, we believe in our power again.

Start with something small. For example, maybe you say, "I'm sorry" a lot, when you've done nothing wrong. Or maybe you compulsively check your phone while driving. Or maybe you beat yourself up over small mistakes. Practice stopping, breathing, and returning to the moment. Let the energy of the present flood you with a regenerative force. Warning: we live in a culture that celebrates laziness. You are not your culture. Use the power of your conviction to repeatedly push against your patterned norm until you break through to a new norm. Train your mind to see what's going right and track your wins. This will help you win more. Be patient. Once you start seeing results, you can start making bigger changes. Soon, you'll be redesigning your whole brain.

I am the master of my fate; I am the captain of my soul.
WILLIAM ERNEST HENLEY

GRATITUDE

One more time: your brain is programmed to help you survive; it is not programmed so you'll be happy. Nor is your brain against you being happy. It's just more compelled to keep you alive, regardless of how happy you are while you're alive. Since people traditionally find happy individuals more enjoyable to be around, more magnetic, and more charismatic, I am interested in giving you as many happiness tools as possible. Your brain keeps you alive, your soul steers that life. For those souls interested in reaching destination: happiness, I suggest a gratitude practice.

Do you like the word "gratitude," or is it soft cotton, void of any real meaning for you? How about the words "God" and "love"? We know "gratitude," "God," and "love" are fine words. They stand for phenomenal concepts, but I'm afraid they've been overused and misused to the point of meaninglessness for many of us. These words are like the perfect skin caress that was once sublime but with repetitive, unconscious stimulation now feels numb at best, irritating at worst.

With that said, you know what I mean when I say gratitude. To make sure my words are not lost on you, do me a favor and *feel* what gratitude feels like. Take the time to do it until you are really *feeling* grateful. Maybe you feel the heart-pleasure-body-warm-tingle-fullness thing when you think of your pet or your dreamy, yellow curtains. Maybe you feel it when you think about some unexpectedly nice something someone did. Or maybe you get the gratitude rush when you recognize that *you. are. existing.* Whatever it is that makes you *feel* grateful, once you're there, ask yourself how you got there. What did you do to feel this warm, regenerative, contentment-inducing feeling?

If you read the "Brain" section above and thought, "Hmmm . . . I'm not sure which patterned rut to reroute," then start a gratitude journal. Crafting your brain to feel gratitude instead of lack is one of the best things you can do for your happiness quotient. The reason the word "gratitude" (and probably "love" and "God") has been so overused is that it is so powerful. Everyone's doing it these days. Sometimes what everyone's doing is not sane, but in this instance I agree with Nike: "Just do it!"

THE WAY OF THE SEVEN-STEP GRATITUDE JOURNAL

1. Buy journal.

2. Keep journal by bed.

3. Begin journal with brief documentation about what's going on in your life and how you currently feel.

4. Every night before sleeping and every morning upon waking write ten things you are grateful for.

5. Repeat this practice religiously for three to five weeks.

6. Complete journal by documenting how you feel now and in what ways your life has changed.

7. Continue your gratitude journaling process until you reach your grave (even if the only "journal" you continue to "write" in is your heart)!

> *Grateful people are offered opportunities*
> *and are people magnets.*
> DANI JOHNSON

Don't want to make a journal or do a seven-step anything? No problem. Just bless. Bless. Bless. Bless. Bless your water bottle. Bless your cat. Bless your hard drive. Bless your toenails. Bless your friend. Bless your salmon. Bless what she said. Bless what he said. Bless where you've been. Bless where you are. Bless your doubt. Bless your sadness. Bless your growth. Bless your stagnancy. Bless the wind. Bless your joy. Bless your toilet seat. Bless your back-yard (bless its dirt). Bless your veins. Bless your books. Bless your reading glasses. Bless this moment. Whatever it is, bless it.

3. THE BODY

The hot sun and the total absence of water made the mouth feel as though it were stuffed with cotton. Endurance was part of the sacrificial side of the dance. I did make it through three hot, exhausting days and nights. Thirty pounds of mostly water melted off my lanky twenty-three-year-old frame. I now had a much better sense of who I was, of courage, of the importance of my life, of what I might be able to teach others.

TOM JOHNSON, WRITING ABOUT THE
SHOSHONE SUN DANCE, 1967

I can relate to Johnson's experience. At twenty-one years of age, I too chose to go through my own sacred ordeal.* Staying up into the sunrise, night after night after night. To the left and right of me, chiffon-clad women taken by dance, offering joy in hand gestures and song. The sweat, dirt, fire and countless hours, footprint after footprint, etched into sand. *Know me,* I spoke silently with each footprint. *Remember my signature, the curve of toe, my commitment to meet you each time I pound my body into you.* That ordeal and the ones I have chosen since take all I have to make it through the dark nights. Much like Johnson, I must become Great if I want to survive.

You can find an "ordeal ritual" in almost every indigenous culture around the world, and for good reason. If we persevere beyond the pain at the edge of our limits, we discover we are more powerful than we thought. Once a boy; after an Ordeal, a man. Our industrialized culture is founded on the premise that an easy, comfortable life is a good life, but this has a cost: Our fear of discomfort limits what we attempt to do, so we never find out what we are capable of. We never know how great we really are. How can you be confident in your amazing human abilities if you have never risen to the demands of an ordeal outside the status quo?

---

* I am forever grateful to my Fire family. You know who you are.

A friend of mine made the empowered choice to birth at home. At 5'3" and with hips like a skinny adolescent, she knew this could be the most painful experience of her life, but instead of opting for a hospital setting, with painkilling epidurals and the option of a Cesarean, she trusted herself and her midwife. "Once you do this, you'll know you can do anything. You'll be able to take on wildcats!" Her prelabor pains rendered her unable to sleep for a full week before the birth. She wanted to give up, but when her baby finally emerged, she was fully awake, drug-free, and aware of her greatness. The pain did not kill her. She became great to rise to her ordeal.

Most enlightenment practices focus on transforming suffering. In order to do so, you have to face it head on. How do we face the suffering? With allowance. Another dear friend, Amber Hartnell, "allowed" her birthing contractions so fully that she began to orgasm. She then shared the experience of her orgasmic birth on numerous news and talk shows, beginning a birthing revolution around the world. Allowance brings grace in the midst of extraordinary pain. What Amber discovered went way beyond childbirth. She later had two root canals without anesthesia.

Peacocks purposely eat poison, but the poison doesn't kill them. Instead, it makes their feathers more colorful. Pain is an integral part of being alive. When you know that a certain pain will not destroy you, why not sit back and enjoy it? Surround yourself with the safety you need, then relax into the pain.

One of my strongest pain teachers are clusters of migraine headaches that mysteriously come on daily for three weeks, almost every fall. My body rejects pain medication with a physical allergy, so during those three weeks, I learn from pain. Sometimes I experience five migraines in a single night. If you've ever had a migraine, you know it is not an exalted headache or a stomachache. Each one is a beast of flashing, piercing, screaming sensations.

I've developed a pain-management system to tame this beast or at least stay in the ring with it. At the barest hint of blood-vessel spasming I stop what I'm doing and focus my attention on it. I watch for edges and peaks. I accompany the pain through the corridors and hallways of my skull. I mingle with it like a vampire and princess might mingle with each other: not exactly easy escorts, but vital with alert thrill. I ride the sharp bites, stick through the high-pitch point, wait for the submission, and then, I give thanks. The tight corridors of pain lift, and I'm free to wander again. By cultivating stillness while mingling with the magnitude of sensation, I can cut the duration and strength of the headaches in half.

When we resist pain, whether emotional or physical, it is highly unpleasant. We don't want it. We want pleasure, crave it, beg for it. Our bodies feel pleasure as safety. So how can we stay with our pain and allow it instead of repelling its overwhelming sensation? Would you believe me if I said pain is not possible unless you resist it? What if I told you that pain and pleasure are the same thing? Could it be possible that each is only an extreme sensation, and the way we choose to feel it marks our experience as painful or pleasurable?

A person with charisma is often described as someone who *glows*. So I thought, "What in nature glows naturally, and how does it do it?" Naturally, I thought of the sun. What I discovered about the sun's light-making process floored me. Here's the simple of it: Through heat, gravity, and grace, atoms within the sun connect so completely that they unify. In their unification, it takes less energy to hold them together than when they were separate particles. The excess energy is released into space in the form of sunlight. All the light you have ever experienced is literally the result of connection! Likewise, your pain dissolves when you fuse it with acceptance, releasing that special glow. Through deep allowance and surrender, your pain will transform from a prison into a radiant surge of charisma.

Next time pain comes knocking on your front door, choose from the following menu options:

- **THE FEARFUL CHOICE:** Try to push away or ignore the intruder. Warning: Pain doesn't typically disappear when you turn your back on it. It will find other ways to express itself, through your words, movements, actions, and health. Pain unmet is sh——t that piles up inside, fooling you into believing you are made of bad stuff.

- **THE CHARISMATIC CHOICE:** Transform your pain into light by greeting it. Explore it. How much curiosity can you bring to the sensation? How close can you get to it? How much can you allow yourself to embrace pain? Remember, there is a lightning bolt of grace hidden in every now. Get good at standing your ground, and you may find the clouds of pain mysteriously dissolving into personal radiance.

   To get acquainted with your pain threshold, here are a couple of baby steps. Try them often. Repetition paves the way to pain-free pain:

- **TAKE A SHOWER:** At the beginning of a shower, while the water is warming up, most people let the cold water run down the drain. But hey! That's the best part! Don't ever waste that cold shower again. Jump right in and be delivered to the kingdom of Intense Sensation. You may enjoy it so much that later, after your body gets to soak in heat (make it so hot your skin turns a nice, healthy, rosy red), you turn that shower handle 180 degrees, back to ice cold again!

   Not only will this wake you up better than warmth, it requires you to open up to the uncomfortable sensation. You will discover that the more you resist, the more uncomfortable you become. Keep reminding your reactionary reptilian mind that neither the superhot nor the supercold water is hurting you. If your tissues start curling in on themselves like sea anemones, deep breaths focused on opening them will provide the needed reminder.

Beyond being an awesome way to get into the moment, this invigorating shower play is great for your health! Alternating hot and cold water submersions will get your lymph moving and your circulation racing while rolling your depression right down the drain. Test it out for yourself. Today is as good a time as any.

- **WALK ON GRAVEL:** Take your shoes off, find a nice stretch of gravelly rock, and walk. Like hot and cold showers, the intense sensations of gravel-walking pulls you promptly into the present. Beyond that, walking on gravel stimulates all of the acupressure points on the bottom of your feet.

  Speaking of pain points, acupuncture is another excellent presence-cultivation practice. I've had many a transcendent moment on the acupuncture table. Needles, gravel, ice, staying up all night—what a close friend calls "Robin's Torture-Your-Way-to-Health program." I call this my "Feel-Your-Way-Into-Now" program. The gift of bodily sensation is that it happens right now!

- **HAVE SEX:** Go get some nookie. (Twist your arm, right?) On your own or with a partner, gently, attentively, consciously explore how your body and mind react to staying in the moment during sexual stimulation. This is easier said than done.

  Internet pornography is a raging phenomenon that removes the individual from his or her immediate circumstances during arousal, and, with the immediate availability of online porn, erectile dysfunction is at an all-time high among college-aged men.[5] Sounds implausible, right? But when confronted with an actual partner, more and more young men just can't get into the moment. And that's just the guys.

Many women struggle with fully experiencing sexual pleasure, going years into their adulthood without ever having an orgasm. Scientists have measured the physical arousal in female participants versus their perceived mental and emotional experience. For many of the participants, although their bodies registered signals of healthy sexual arousal, the women reported experiencing no sensations.[6] They did not feel what their bodies were responding to.

> *The clitoris is pure in purpose.*
> *It is the only organ in the body designed*
> *purely for pleasure.*
> EVE ENSLER, *THE VAGINA MONOLOGUES*

While pain is nothing more than a resistance to extreme sensation, pleasure is a direct product of allowance. If you want to experience the wonders of being alive, ask yourself, "How much feeling can I pay attention to?" When you feel like you're shutting down or vacating the premises, stop yourself, overcome fear, and sink into the moment. Go back to your edge, where sensation calls, and lovingly continue the adventure.

In sum: *Life is poetry, not math.* If you are "nailed" to a cross, this does not mean you are in a bad place or that *you* are bad. However, it does require you to reach for a greater power than the one that got you nailed there.

You will be nailed to a cross, or you will nail yourself to one. It's bound to happen. Once you're there, you can wither and writhe, tearing your flesh further with your squirming, angry resistance, or you can use the hurt as an opening to stop, listen, and *feel*. It will go against every *animal instinct* in you pressing to break free. Your *angel instinct* has its own approach. Still looking to "set yourself free," your *angel instinct* opens the widest loving eyes and looks directly into your hurt. Every time you follow your angel instinct and face your hurt, instead of running, you open the faucet for a great power to come through.

4. THE SPIRIT

While you are here with me, drink plenty of water.
And please remember to remember with every sip,
you are actually drinking clouds.

THICH NHAT HANH

The final frontier of your journey to confidence is in your connection with Spirit. Once you have begun to redesign your brain-scape and to overcome your fear of pain, you'll probably be feeling a new kind of inner strength: a certain pride and faith in yourself. You know, confidence. It is with this new confidence that you can begin breathing magic back into the details. Remember the curiosity and reverence the animists felt for every rock and tree? Remember your childhood joy the first time you held a puppy? It's time to bring back that curiosity and joy.

Start with food. Go to the grocery store. Before placing any item in your cart, look for its *value*. What's valuable about this banana? That can of mushrooms? Those lobster legs? Try it out. I'm about to tell you one of the biggest keys to cultivating charisma. This is not the last time we will discuss this first charisma tool. It goes like this: *Whenever you choose to look for value, you accentuate your charisma.*

Say grace before dinner. Saying grace has nothing to do with whether or not you are religious. When you say grace, you bless your food before making it a part of you, which can only be a good thing. You might start by hovering the portals of your palms a few inches above your plate, feeling for the food's life force, while sending some of your own into the morsels you're about to eat. Then give that meal a good talkin' to:

Hey, there, pretty red beets and purple squash! What up lima bean and turkey thigh? Gotta say, your heated flesh rising as hot steam from your marjoram and thyme sure do smell good!

I'm so grateful for the functioning of my superorganism hive, whose collaboration allows me to share this candlelit moment with you. It doesn't get more intimate than what we're about to do.

Yes, I'm going to eat you.

I hope it's as good for you as it is for me.

And you, my pretty lima bean, I'd like to offer you to my friend over here. You'll love her lips.

Where, why, and when did we lose the shocking intimacy of our physicality? Masticating lettuce, tomato, and potato. The jostle of patella and meniscus. It's not only food. Branch out. Start to see value in the foliage around you, in the gum on the bench, between the cracks in the pavement, in the hallelujah in the slide of your soap. The more you look for something, the more that thing becomes part of you. Look for value in all things, and you may start to reverse-engineer It.

Charisma has been depicted for millennia through artists' renditions of halos—radiating golden orbs that glow around the heads and bodies of various spiritual, celebrity, and religious figures. By relating to the vibrant, vital essence of your food, your water, your friends, your news stories, spirit in plastic speakers, spirit in plastic Barbies, God in All of the Stuff, you will start to grow your very own holy halo. *You become what you relate to.*

In Eastern Orthodox Christianity, deification of oneself, known as theosis, is highly esteemed. The goal of theosis is nothing less than expressing the "state of God" or "likeness of God" through union with God.

(THE)OSIS: THE- [GOD] + -OSIS [STATE]

It gets better. One day I was reading a book by neuroscientists Andrew Newberg and Mark Robert Waldman called *How God*

Changes Your Brain. Specifically, I was reading the research results in a chapter entitled, "What Does God Feel Like?" Newberg and Waldman had traveled the world over, studying everyone from nuns to Buddhist monks to Candomblé practitioners to source their answers. Here's what they had to say:

> Returning to our analysis of the survey participants' descriptions [of spiritual experience], we began to group different words into different types of categories. By far the largest category included words that reflected strong emotional content. Nearly a third described their [spiritual] experiences as being intense, using words like ecstatic, powerful, exhilarating, and profound. Nearly one-half described their experiences using words that expressed calmness, serenity, and contentment. This correlates well with our neurological model suggesting that spiritual experiences simultaneously stimulate the sympathetic (arousing) and parasympathetic (calming) nervous systems. Generally speaking, it is rare that an experience both arouses and calms.[7]

Suddenly, I got excited. I pulled out the results of my own poll, entitled: "What Does Charisma Feel Like?" I read over a couple of examples:

- "Calmly magnetic and radiantly exciting."
- "Strong and warm."

"Uh huh," I thought and turned to another page in *How God Changes Your Brain*, running my eyes along random responses from the researchers and their subjects:

> "Many people experienced God as a way of connecting to the universe, to nature, and with others."
> "God gave me a vision of who I am."
> "The world became more three-dimensional. More intense, rich and pleasurable."

"I also felt an openness, positive feeling, gratitude, unconditional regard, etc., for all things and people. As though I'd encountered the Golden Rule, love of neighbor as myself, concretely within this moment. These feelings or instances of awareness were intuitive and implicit—that is, they seemed to come without actual thoughts or words."[8]

Something clicked. I looked back at my "charisma" poll and read further down to another bullet point list:

- "It provides a sense of purpose and hope as if anything is possible."
- "It takes others on a ride. A rich larger-than-life ride."
- "I feel accepted. Like I'm invited to be me. In fact, I feel greater than normal around it!"
- "It's a natural ability to connect."
- "It uplifts, enriches and enlarges others."
- "It's searing presence."
- "It provides whatever's needed in the moment."
- "It's that thing about somebody that just glows."
- "It's the ability to claim space."
- "It's personality magic."
- "It's soul power."
- "It's confidence."
- "I don't know. Does anybody know what charisma is?"

The similarities were too strong to be coincidental. It's almost as if the cultivation of charisma allows you to give godly experiences! While you're taking that in, imagine this: Dr. Newberg and Dr. Waldman go on to say,

> Religious and spiritual contemplation changes your brain in a profound way because it strengthens a unique neural circuit that specifically enhances social awareness and empathy while subduing destructive feelings and emotions.[9]

And then,

> New dendrites will rapidly grow and old associations will disconnect as new imaginative perspectives emerge. In essence, when you think about the really big questions in life—be they religious, scientific, or psychological—your brain is going to grow.[10]

That's right. By engaging in "God" questions, wondering what *banged* the big bang, or contemplating what was before the Word, you are getting smarter and more sociable. You are redesigning your brain. You are both calming and invigorating yourself. Allow yourself to ask the big questions and watch any remaining self doubt melt away like an ice cube in hot tea.

What's Your Calling?

There is a high correlation between confidence and purpose. Whether or not you believe in destiny, you know the difference between feeling passionately engaged in life versus robotic and gray. To repeat the words of Tony Robbins, "Passion wakes you up to something in life that you desire so strongly that you no longer have to push yourself to do anything. You now have a different kind of drive; a force that pulls you forward."[11] People spend eons searching to be pulled forward by their passion. Find it, and you have found your *calling*. Find your calling and you have found something worthy of the time it takes to become a master. As you develop mastery, you develop your *confidence*.

Fine, Robin, fine. But how???

Listen.

Listen for your inspired heart.

Listen for your design and make up.

Listen for the gifts that are built into your sinews.

Listen for the passion that pulls you to give them.

What work makes you feel alive? Which places give you

vitality? Who brings you to life? Arrange your days around this work, these places, and these people.

Take note: What makes you alive today may be different tomorrow. Like life, your calling does not stagnate. Only death does that. You have a calling. *Listen* for your inspired heart so you can follow "Greatness" *in* its footsteps.

Humans are quite possibly the only creatures who can be physically in one place while our senses and "what-if" imagination are somewhere else. Born into this split-mind condition, we must make time to exist in a carefree, fully sensed way, however briefly, each and every day. Make room for what's *happening*.

Every second, this time-encased room burns to ashes, waiting to clear the traffic lights and open the way. Place your identity not in rooms; place it at the edges of discovery. You cannot *lead* from the past, from a closed room; you can lead from now, from the open edge.

Learn to court the extraordinary. Spend time in the dark. If it gets to be too much, seek the gratitude inside yourself, and grow it so you can one day hold the numinous. Follow your calling. Leave the closed rooms of the past, and seek the edge of the road as it opens.

Like death, it will come in its own time.

Like life, it will leave you wanting more.

CALLED-OUT BY A BILLIONAIRE

In 2001, Sanjiv Sidhu was the richest person of Indian origin in the world. He acquired his wealth by inventing innovative supply chain management software and services. The result: he saved companies a lot of money in gas and resources while simultaneously saving the planet from the aftermath of such wastes. I met Sanjiv where I meet most everyone of vital importance to me—on the dance floor, using the language beyond words. Years later, I interviewed Sanjiv about work, success, and finding one's calling.

Sanjiv: A lot of people these days are saying, "Do what you really enjoy! Just follow your passion!" So everyone wants to be a rock star and no one wants to be a janitor. No one wants to work in a factory because it's mind numbing. But it doesn't have to be. I have always focused on what people needed and then found a way to fulfill that need. I consider this a service-oriented way of listening for your calling. I would think to myself, "People need this so I'll really enjoy doing it. And ultimately, I always would."

It's a great privilege when it turns out that what you most want to do also serves the needs of others. But sometimes it just doesn't work out that way. In those moments, look to see how you can fulfill the needs of others instead of your own—you may become pleasantly surprised to discover personal satisfaction along the way. The satisfaction bit will come from doing the job. You can't usually see it coming ahead of time. Simply dive in and trust! You won't know where the wave can take you until you hop on. Choose something and engage with it furiously. If it's a business idea, try to sell it. Once you sell it keep modifying the product, the sales process, and your perspective until it becomes what you refer to as a "Calling."

Meanwhile, look to find balance in everything. Like the Buddha says, take the middle path. If you see the demand is for people to slaughter animals and that's not aligned with your values, than no matter how high the demand, slaughtering animals is not going to work out so well. It's about balance; I think the follow your heart message has gone too far. It's become "the destination is the award" versus. "no matter what you are doing you can make it fulfilling by enjoying the fruits that will come as you serve others."*

BIT-SIZED BILLIONAIRE WISDOM
Listen for your Calling in what people and the planet are calling for.

---

* To practice becoming empowered despite circumstances, visit Sanjiv Sidhu's website, www.Version2.me

Conclusion

It's time to break down the myth of science versus the mystical unknown. Instead of seeing these perspectives as being at odds with each other, we could be treating science as a valuable sidekick in our quest for joy and revelation. Thank you, science, for creating tools for our explorations! As my friend Dr. Joshua Levin says,

> It is science that has helped us to understand that we are truly one race, one people, with essentially the same biology and potentials. It is the scientific way of discovery that invites us to each question how it is that we have come to believe. For some beliefs are powerful effective tools for living, growing, loving, and creating in the world. Some beliefs lead to health and wellbeing, and some lead to hell on earth.

The role of science is to keep asking questions. As it trains the eyes of telescope and microscope in search of truth, science is always ready to be proven wrong; it changes its theories all the time in light of new discoveries. But many of us humans, tail between our legs in the face of change, have trouble allowing both science and religion to grow. We want science to explain away the unknown with hard facts. We want religion to comfort us in the unknown by giving us faith. Science is not the problem. Spirituality is not the problem. The problem, my friend, is our fear of change, surprise, and uncertainty—our fear of the unknown. But the unknown is the e-ticket ride, baby. It's the Space Mountain in the Disneyland of life, and, by it's very nature, it will never be explained. None of the big questions have answers. The life force within us is a scientific mystery. Our thoughts and emotions are barely probed, magical fields of inquiry. What makes you want to splash a puddle of rain? What started this big, blossoming chain of events that led to right now? Sorry, folks, we have no answers. Whatever animates this universe is a big fat question mark.

So what are we left with? Evolutionary theory, the great sciences, religion, mysticism, and philosophy all point to an intelligence that moves through each life form, transforming it in minuscule ways in every moment. Some might understand this transformational intelligence as that which etches deep character lines, like signatures, onto eighty-eight-year-old faces. Others might understand it as the force that transforms a hard little coiled acorn into a magnificent oak tree. Even that mighty oak was once just some nut, and that nut didn't make itself grow into an oak tree. It allowed itself to become an oak tree. Whatever force did the growing is beyond the understanding of science. So, was it God?

The general culture of today holds God in quarantine, waiting for the verdict to come in. Is she/he/it real or is she/he/it fake? In a climate where rationalism rules, skepticism comes before believing. Carl Sagan, America's favorite scientist and religious skeptic during the last century, was not a believer per se, yet he still held God as unknown,[12] so the answer is still, "Maybe."

We don't know. Whatever banged all of us into being must be untouchable. Yet we must be touching it when we touch our lover's hand or a perfect green pea. There is something that we may never be able to measure, certainly not into dependable fractions and facts. Thank God! I mean really, the ineffable magnitude of what's possible in the face of all we don't know is simply thrilling!

Ever stood alone in the middle of a great redwood forest? Or hung out in the silence beneath a wave as it crashes over your body? Our hearts mourn the magic that was lost to us when we let our disenchanted culture dictate life as solely factual, controllable, and mechanical. Let's take that magic back. Reclaim your right to be inexplicable, to probe and question the sensations of what's banging you into being. The more you look directly into your self the more your value will shine, and it will come with a straighter spine.

"The Son of God
became man
(that would be us),
that we might
become God
(Lettin' it happen
over here)!"

ST. ATHANASIUS OF ALEXANDRIA
(WITH MY COMMENTARY)

KNOW YOUR VALUE.

STEP TWO
MAGNETISM
Show Your Value

CHARISMA RULE
Show the world the great stuff you're made of.

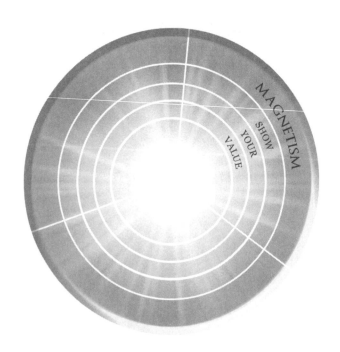

Ruby's an "It" dog. She has that hard-to-define quality—that charm, that goofiness, that joie de vivre—that wins minds and melts hearts. Simply put, whatever that "It" is, she's got it.

FOSTER DOG ADOPTION AD, 2014

IT

In the early 1900s, the word "charisma" was used only in the realm of charismatic Christianity.* However, as the American vaudeville era gave way to cinema, pop culture created a new term to describe people who were known for giving exceptional gifts of grace. These people were described as having "It."

The word "It" rose to prominence quickly. Its simplicity seemed to capture the intangible nature of a certain special something. For example, in 1904, Rudyard Kipling wrote: "It isn't beauty, so to speak, nor good talk necessarily. It's just 'It.'"[1] Elinor Glyn, who wrote the original magazine story that inspired the silent film *It*, starring the original "It girl," Clara Bow, wrote: "It" is that quality possessed by some which draws all others with its magnetic force. With "It" you win all men if you are a woman and all women if you are a man."[2]

Not long after, in 1927, Miss Mary Pickford became the first film actress to be called "America's sweetheart." During her heyday, one fan described Pickford this way: "She is blessed with magnetic personality—that indescribable something—which colors and vitalizes everything she does."[3] Mary Pickford had It.

"It" is not defined by gender, race, age, or income. You may have the perfect waist-to-bust ratio, a fabulous hair flip, the fastest car, or the biggest ding-dong, but it don't mean a thing if you ain't got that . . . It. Magnetism isn't bought, sold, or stolen. We're talking about the spark that draws you to conventionally unattractive actors like Steve Buscemi and Philip Seymour Hoffman, or that one unabashedly dorky girl in high school whom everyone

---

* Also known as Spirit-filled Christianity.

loved. "It" is the ability to fearlessly express your inner self for the whole world to see.

Mary Pickford's advice column *Daily Talks* reminded readers that the most attractive people were those who learned to "be themselves." Mary Pickford didn't own It, like you own good hair or a slick sports car. Instead she "colored and vitalized everything she did" with the power of *herself*. She filled every moment with signature Mary Pickford. She gave her gifts. If you're wishing you had It too, you're going to love this chapter!

You've reached stage two of your charisma training. If you've been practicing what I'm preaching, you are already beginning to do the following:

BODY

- Quiet a ruminating mind by becoming absorbed in the physical sensations of your body—both the painful ones and the pleasure-filled ones. (Take cold showers, gravel walk, have sex.)

- In other words, train your body and mind to mingle with and allow intense sensations. (Do not push away; let in.)

- Induce an ordeal that will force you to move beyond your comfort zone, thus showing you how great and resourceful you are. (If you experience migraines or are going to go into labor, you've got more than enough material to begin to move beyond your comfort zone.)

MIND

- Carefully guide your questioning mind towards "What if" questions that support your worth and encourage your authenticity. (*What if I'm enough?*)

- Repattern your neural pathways towards happiness. (Keep a gratitude journal, ask the questions that will help you reverse-engineer the life you want, and don't forget to play.)

- Challenge your beliefs to decide which to keep and which to rewire. (Are humans inherently sinful? Is there really a right from wrong? Are some things good and some things bad?)

SPIRIT

- Integrate play into your day. (Get a trampoline, maybe join a rough-and-tumble wrestling club, dance, joke, wonder, fall down, get up.)

- Discover your inherent value, speak a language beyond words, and grow smarter by questioning what all things are made of. (What banged the big bang? "In the beginning was the Word" (John 1:1). Before the Word was . . . THE.)

- Look for the value in all objects—animate and inanimate.

- When you find you're in a rut, gain perspective by stargazing or entering the wilderness

- Listen for your calling and dedicate yourself to it. (Sometimes your calling will sing to you from your heart. Sometimes it will cry out through what others need. If you're lucky, your calling will passionately make itself known from both your inner world and the outer world. One way or the other, be fearless following it.)

By golly, you are now officially awesome! Your confidence is growing, and you're ready to embark on step two: Magnetism.

Cultivating magnetism requires a two-pronged approach. First, you must love yourself so madly that your natural authority fills the room. Second, you must grow yourself into a god. Do those two steps frighten you? Are you beginning to wonder if I'm advocating narcissism? Well, wonder no more, because I am. Read on. I'll explain it all in a bit.

Meanwhile, it's sufficient to know that the combination of two ingredients—loving who you are now and growing yourself into a god—come together to produce the unique ingredient you offer humanity's stone soup: your boldest self. Fearless expression of your dynamic persona is magnetic and will not only set you free; it frees those around you. Why? Because freedom is contagious. Everyone wants to be free. They just need permission.

Have you ever been in a meeting and wished you could just speak up, but when you mentally reviewed what you wanted to say, your whole body went weak? Next thing you realize you've officially missed the window of opportunity to contribute. Moments like these feel anything but victorious. They feel frustrating. And they do not help you build your confidence or magnetism. This chapter will help you speak up, show up, and turn your glow up.

1. FIRST HALF: LOVING YOURSELF INTO AN AUTHORITY

I was bringing myself as though I were a basket of flowers!
KATHARINE HEPBURN

Magnetism is the ability to elicit love from others. When someone is magnetic, we don't think of them as attracting just anything (e.g., squirrels, dirt, or the police). Rather, we say someone is magnetic because we can't help but love them immediately, illogically, and irresistibly. You want that too?

The first step to cultivating magnetism is creating the habit of letting love in. The best and only surefire way to make certain you are an easy target for love is to love yourself. Love is a like-attracts-like sort of a thing. Think about the most magnetic people you know, the people who seem to draw others to them like bees to honey, moths to flame, flies to horse dung. Are they actively hiding their gifts in a cloak of slouched embarrassment, or are they embracing the goods they've got with sure swagger? The answer is obvious. Self-love is a prerequisite for magnetism.

Unfortunately, cultural prejudices make practicing self-love easier said than done. I'll show you what I mean.

Every day, the beautiful Narcissus came to the lake. There, he knelt down to gaze at his reflection. So enraptured was Narcissus with his own beauty, that he fell in love with himself. The gods, disgusted by Narcissus's self-obsession, turned him into a flower. To this day, the white narcissus grows by the banks of the river.

The story of Narcissus told this way suggests that self-love is a terrible sin, worthy of punishment. The term "narcissist," which comes from this myth, is listed in the DSM-IV[4] (the psychological bible) as a serious psychiatric disorder, but is it? Let's use our alchemical "What if?" and see what happens. What if the same story were told a little differently?

A beautiful young man named Narcissus knew his own beauty and celebrated it daily. The gods, seeing his joy and radiance, preserved Narcissus's joy eternally by making his beauty immortal. They transformed him into a pure and lovely blossom, and to this day, he blooms as the narcissus flower for all the world's delight.

Surely this is a happier way to think about self-love. Let me take a second to blow your mind. When we call someone a narcissist, words like "arrogant" and "selfish" arise. We imagine that the people in question are withholding their gifts (eg., attention, praise, goods, and status) from us. When we don't see them giving us their love, we assume they are keeping that love for themselves. Then, as members of the deeply interconnected human superorganism, we resent them for it.

This logic doesn't make sense. You can't withhold love; it's infectious. You cannot give love away unless you've got love to give. Once you're filled up with It, you can't help but spill that love all over the place! This is the glow no plastic surgeon or youth cream can bring. Think of the last time you found yourself pleasantly and contentedly in love with yourself—maybe at your birthday party or after a long day of good work. Did you hoard your stuff, or did you give it away? There is no such beast as the narcissist who hovers over his or her own love like a dragon guarding gold. That's not love, folks. It's fear.

Our cultural archetype of the Narcissist is based on a major misconception. When people seem arrogant, selfish, or self-involved, they aren't in love with themselves. More likely, they are trapped in a painful cycle of self-repression, too afraid to shine their soul's jewelry or not knowing how. Scared to show themselves, they hide, building impenetrable walls of defense. Of course, these walls won't keep pain out. They merely stop the builders from giving their gifts and being able to receive gifts from others. These people can't experience love from anyone, because they don't love themselves. It's a self-defeating cycle, cloaked by the illusion of self-sufficiency. Newsflash: If you're a human being with human emotions, then I'm sorry, self-sufficiency will never work for you. You need people, and they need you. Start loving yourself so you can spill that love all over the place, because this is how our species is designed to survive.

The most successful people I know are not the most conceited. They are so full of grace and abundance, they can't help but overflow to everyone around them. Of course people are magnetized to them! Self-love is not the opposite of generosity; it is the prerequisite for it.

CULTURE AND THE BATTLE FOR SELF-LOVE

Once you make the choice to love yourself unconditionally, be prepared for some initial cultural backlash. Pay attention; this backlash is subtle and requires immediate attention.

Like oxygen, culture is invisible—and just as necessary for our survival. As an anthropologist and traveler, I've learned that each culture demands its own unique set of behaviors. What is celebrated in one land is condemned in another.

Western culture has deep-rooted issues with self-love. There is a chocolate box of explanations for this, not the least of which is our society's early Greek roots. To this day, Greek myths like the tale of Narcissus are embedded in the cultural air we breathe. They subliminally affect all of our decisions, from what to wear (if anything at all) to our choice of mates and careers. Tales are woven deeply into our moral tapestry, and the story of Narcissus isn't the only Greek myth to warn us about getting uppity.*

TALE NUMBER ONE

Icarus and his pop were prisoners on top of a building in Crete, so they fabricated a couple of sets of wax wings to escape. Before they set off in flight, Icarus's father said: "Don't fly too high; the sun will melt your wings." Once in the air, Icarus was overcome by the glorious sensation of flight and flew as close to the sun as he could. As his father had warned, the sun melted his wings; Icarus plummeted into the sea and drowned.

Cultural Mythos Message: *Better not fly too high. Stay with everyone else.*

TALE NUMBER TWO

The titan Prometheus gave the secret of fire to humans. When Zeus discovered this, he punished Prometheus by tying him to a rock in the middle of the ocean. Each and every day, an eagle came and ate his liver. At night, Prometheus's liver regenerated in preparation for the eagle's next daily meal. His suffering is said to continue for eternity.

---

* Big thanks to the brilliant neuropsychologist Dr. Mario Martinez for first drawing my attention to the following three tales and their influence on humanity's current cultural beliefs around "Greatness."

Cultural Mythos Message: Don't dare offer anything new, great, or powerful, because there will be consequences. Scale down your innovations and obey the status quo, or suffer eternal, excruciating pain.

TALE NUMBER THREE

King Sisyphus brought the secret of immortality to man. In punishment, Zeus made him roll a giant boulder up a hill. Each time Sisyphus neared the summit, the boulder rolled back down. Again, the torture lasts for eternity.

Cultural Mythos Message: Ditto Prometheus. Nothing new, great, or powerful, or you will be punished. Hide your genius!

Every culture makes stories to explain and maintain its way of life. We find similar examples of these Greek-myth messages warning us not to get too big or too high, throughout much of the world. In Japan, this concept is spread with the common Japanese proverb "The peg that sticks out will be hammered down." In Australia and New Zealand, you will hear about the "tall poppy syndrome," wherein those people who grow into their greatness are cut down via envy and resentment from their peers. Before literacy caught on, oral history was (and in some places still is) the only way to pass information from one generation to the next. This included essential, real-life stuff, like where to find water, which lizards not to eat, and the rules of social life. Knowing this, it's easy to conclude that Narcissus and the other "Greatness"-fearing tales were used for an important reason. Perhaps they were intended to foster a cohesive society of agreeable, obedient people, who wouldn't create surprises for the guys up top. Maybe they were a way of dealing with our fear of the unknown, or maybe they were created to deal with another powerful fear: the fear of failure. Whatever the initial reason, these myths insist that the safe way to "deal" is by staying small.

Our human brains are hardwired to remember stories, and those stories subconsciously guide us through our world of relationships and resources. In America, we no longer rely on our grandfolks' yarns. Today storytelling through television and cinema is a huge part of our lives, reenforcing our ideas of what is lovable and what is not. As Thom Hartmann, author of *The Last Hours of Ancient Sunlight* says, "Culture is not about what is absolute, real, or true. It's about what a group of people get together and agree to believe. Culture can be healthy or toxic, nurturing or murderous. Culture is made of stories."[5]

A lot has changed since ancient Greece, but the baggage we carry from our robe-and-sandal-clad ancestors still leads to insane patterns of conceit and jealousy. Instead of praising people who have the qualities we desire, we often feel insecure around them, and then we deflect praise that should regenerate us. Ever denied a compliment? I'll bet you have. I bet you were trying to be "modest."

The word "culture" comes from Latin, *cultura*, and literally means "cultivation," a concept based on a term first used by the Roman orator Cicero: *cultura animi*, or "cultivation of the soul." Culture is simply an environment in which to grow something. Human cultural instinct propels us to collaborate and invent, share stories, develop language, build things, initiate and maintain relationships, and stay alive.

Here's a problem for you: What if your culture is growing big problems, like, oh, I don't know . . . widespread hunger? Abuse of resources? High levels of depression and anxiety? I mean, if that is the case, maybe that culture isn't working so well. Culture is, after all, a human invention. It's simply what we choose to grow. *We will grow whatever it is we value.* In my opinion, culture is the coolest thing going. Because of it, we don't have to wait around for evolution's clock to tick random genetic mutations. If we want change, instead of waiting generations for our biology to do it for us, we pass on lightning-quick idea genes called "memes."

Evolutionary biologist Richard Dawkins first coined the word *meme* in his 1976 book, *The Selfish Gene*. In short, a meme is the behavioral equivalent of a gene.

Have an insatiable dream of moving to Iceland? Go. You need not suffer while evolution slowly and painfully figures out the survival logistics of extra fat and fur. Instead, before you even step on Iceland's ice, you'll likely go online, take a look at happy, warm creatures gallivanting in snow, and ask, *"What if* I could do that too? And how?" Voila! You reverse-engineer your survival mechanics with that sexy Russian hat you've had your eye on, your very own insulated snow den, and a faux-fur mink coat. We can use this same formula to alter those greenhouse-gas, doomsday scenarios. Just imagine it better, start at the result, and work backwards!

CULTURE RULES

Culture is what happens when more than one person is present.

ROBERT RICHMAN, AUTHOR OF *THE CULTURE BLUEPRINT*

One: Culture is always in you, even when you are alone, but it requires the star of our show, the currency of connection, to do what it does best. To spread, culture needs two people. It's aching to transmit its idea "genes" from you to someone else. Remember, culture cultivates. It loves to grow.

Two: Culture changes every time you share a thought, every time you post a comment online that is read by another. Culture is changing because you are reading this book.

Three: Culture is our social "DNA," and, in the same way sex works its mixing magic on biological DNA, we mix and shake up our social codes every time we connect.

Four: Want to change culture? Ask, "What if?" and "cultivate'" an answer.

History shows that when an idea is shared by people with great magnetism, it is more likely to go viral and trigger massive influence and change. No matter what the haters say, your self-love is the first step towards making that kind of culture shift. Once you know your value, showing your value is a fairly unconscious byproduct; you don't have to try hard to make it happen. You need buy no flamingo feathers or chartreuse sunglasses. You need not perform a speech in Elvis pasties. You don't even need to think about who you are or if you're showing that person to others. To nourish the sprout of your self-knowing into substantial magnetism, all you need to do is love who you are. As I said, if you are ready to take that step and choose self-love, be prepared for resistance. Cultural expectations will push back, calling you conceited, immodest, self-involved, but you will prevail. Stay strong. It's time to use culture literally. In the way Cicero employed *cultura animi* in classical antiquity, it's time we "cultivate soul."

REBEL (OR, "HOW TO GET THAT SWEET, SWEET LOVIN'")

Okay! Ready to get proactive? Excellent! Another way to talk about loving yourself is to think about becoming your own personal authority. In his book *Charisma: The Gift of Grace and How It Has Been Taken Away from Us,* sociologist and scholar Philip Rieff wrote that he considers "'soul-making' a synonym for 'charisma' that has the rare virtue of revealing more than it obscures, for 'soul' is nothing to us if it does not represent an internalization of personal authority."[6]

Let me tell you a story:

A fella by the name of Dr. Mario Martinez is a clinical psychoneuroimmunologist who researches people over one hundred years old, also called centenarians. At one point, Dr. Martinez realized that all his centenarians had something in common: they were rebels. In other words, they considered themselves to be the primary authority of their own lives. They knew what felt right to them and they did it, regardless of what other people would have them think or do. Here's just one conversation among many that Dr. Martinez reported having with centenarians worldwide:

> "When was the last time you went to a doctor?" asked Dr. Martinez.
>
> "About forty-five years ago," the centenarian replied.
>
> "What does your doctor have to say about that?"
>
> "Well, I don't know, they're all dead."[7]

Learning to navigate the invisible persuasion of your culture is a serious self-loving task. You've gotta become conscious of what it's telling you so you can make a conscious choice to rebel or concede. You have a choice, but you need to know what the options are. In every moment. To do this, you must first become aware of which parts of your culture cultivate your soul, and which parts, if you follow them, will hide It. Taking inventory will help you become a powerhouse of soulful influence, acting from your sovereign seat of empowerment instead of reacting as a robot in a backseat bucket seat.

The first thing you can do is to ask questions, all the time, like a crazy person—questions you never thought to ask. Questions like this:

> When does my culture tell me it's okay to cry? When is it okay to scream?
>
> What am I supposed to wear to weddings? How about on a first date?
>
> What time does my culture tell me to go to bed? Get up in the morning?
>
> What am I supposed to do on a Saturday night? How about on a Sunday?
>
> Should I shake your hand or hug you? How hard and for how long?

Asking fundamental questions about how you decide what you do will get you thinking about what you want and who you are. "Love" is a verb. Your thoughts and actions toward yourself are how you love yourself. Discovering what you want provides information about who you are, and you have to know who you are to love that person.

Your task is to gently pick through your behavior, in the moment, and figure out if you are doing something authentic to you or something you've been told to do. Traveling helps. A lot. Because of my experience with so many different cultures, I can feel the persuasiveness of cultural influence wherever I go. I feel its invisible whisper telling me what to do and what not to do: *Be a nice girl. Don't say no too much. Better Botox those forehead lines . . .* etched in time by God.

The voice of my culture is so ingrained in my head that it often sounds like my own. But it is not. Learning to tell the difference between what culture is telling you to do and what you feel to be correct is vital in knowing who you are, and as I said, knowing who you are is vital to loving yourself. So I invite you: explore your right to be a sovereign human being, and reclaim the authority to cultivate your soul as you see fit.

Once you become aware of how culture influences your actions and desires, you can decide if those actions and desires are right for you. What does your body feel like when you do that culturally accepted thing? Indicators that a cultural norm is healthy for you might include sensations of openness, spaciousness, oxygenation, pleasure, and free-flowing energy. On the flip side, nausea, contraction, and shrinking are indicators that a particular cultural norm is not healthy for you.

Question: What should you do when culture tells you to do something, but your body says stop doing it?

Answer: Stop doing it.

On the other hand, if something feels good, but people in your culture tell you some bull dung about it being "weird" or whatever, they're probably just being robots. People who are afraid to show who they really are respond automatically to difference by pointing it out and tattling on it. Don't worry about them. *Do yo' thang, you sexy, sassy weirdo, you.* Seriously. You will be healthier and happier, and maybe set a new trend! Anything that has ever been cool started out severely uncool. But people felt right doing it, followed their passion, and eventually, the haters realized that they were missing out on a whole lot of fun and joy.

My seventy-nine-year-old stepfather, Howard Stein, has this to say: "Whatever your philosophy is, if it works for you and you don't get aggravated by it, then it's the right way."

Howard is a shining example of charisma. He was born into extreme poverty, to a Jewish mother who loved him unconditionally. In her mind (and subsequently his), there was nothing Howard could do wrong. In high school, six feet tall and 125 pounds, with horrific acne, he recalls asking girls to dance. When they turned him down, he said to himself, "Something must seriously be wrong with that girl."

To this day, Howard Stein can still do no wrong. As a result, he has numerous multi-million-dollar businesses and a beautiful wife. Because Howard Stein believes that everything he touches will turn to gold, it does. Howard has that unconventional attractiveness that comes from believing he's made of great stuff. You know—"It."

Once you get comfortable asking simple questions, start rephrasing them into "What if" questions. For example:

What if I hug you longer?
What if I tell you I don't want to hug you?
What if I wear only a tie when she comes home?
What if I wear pajamas on a first date?
What if I cry on the bus?
What if I rock out on the exercise machine?
What if I never have children?
What if I play with Legos at my desk?

THE POWER OF THE REBEL

By three methods we may learn wisdom: First, by reflection, which is noblest; Second, by imitation, which is easiest; and third by experience, which is the bitterest.

CONFUCIUS

As you begin to grow into your own unique greatness, start asking yourself what you want to contribute to history. This question is not as far-fetched as you might think. If you are doing this work diligently and with passion, your historical relevance is unavoidable. As I've said, our ability to influence our evolution more than any other species is due to our ability to ask questions. Specifically, the question "What if?" Asking "What if?" opens the door to imagining that things could be different, to reverse-engineering our dreams, and consequently, to creating brand new memes.

Memes are ideas transmitted by behavior. They are the *idea-genes* I referred to earlier. Memes can speed up change via the transmission of cultural ideas through the use of language and language beyond words. So,

1. What (and whom) do you mimic? And

2. What outrightly unique you-ness are you bold enough to share?

Everything you do will come from one, the other, or a combination of these two sources. Therefore, your answers to these two questions equal the ingredients you are contributing to our superorganism stone soup.

From a biological standpoint, our species is cradled in incomprehensible freedom of choice. What we think of as "just the way things are," that is, "I've been mimicking my culture/parents/movie stars in this way forever; this is just the way things are," is incorrect. The biological truth is that we direct "the way things are." We direct it every time we mimic a person, idea, or belief or choose instead to pull a unique behavior out of our own treasure of authentic expression.

As *The Charisma Code*'s biologist, Dr. Woolley-Barker, likes to say, "Humans are already providing a platform for new kinds of life (plastic-eating bacteria, domesticated creatures, genetic engineering). Can we do it better? Yes. We can dream a collective dream and reverse-engineer it." Question is, what will you contribute?

What sticks, and therefore creates culture, is dependent on a gazillion factors. For our purposes, it's sufficient to understand that entire revolutions are built from the contagious nature of memes. We are "Ultimate Ecosystem Engineers" and you, my friend, have just as much power to create a meme as any one of your hominid brothers and sisters. As the great social activist and woman I am honored to call friend, Marianne Williamson, recently shared on Oprah's "Super Soul Sunday," "Revolutions always begin with a small group who stand on an idea that's aligned with the ages."

To begin a revolution, you need guts. Guts to stand by your ideas and give them voice. With every act you either show that you value your ideas or show that you don't. Speaking up against the cultural norm is not easy. That's why "Step One, Confidence: *Know Your Value*" is the prerequisite to "Step Two, Magnetism: *Show Your Value*." You think Dr. Martin Luther King Jr. would have stepped in front of a crowd, spouting ideas that he knew made him a bullet target, without first hearing a compelling cry from inside telling him he must? Fearless conviction is bred from knowing your self and the sociopolitical and socioeconomic realities of your environment. Simply put, knowing self and knowing environment are the two necessary prerequisites to "standing on an idea that's aligned with the ages." Fearless expression is what happens when you trust your self enough to act on what you know. Listen up: You have only one tiny window of time on this spinning, blue-green pearl. Activist Russell Brand says it best: "All you're really deciding upon is, do you want to die for something, or do you want to die for nothing?"[8]

If there is one cultural meme this book would like to steer in the other direction, it's the one saying don't get too high, too innovative, too great. Don't fly too close to the sun. The following oft-recited quote from Marianne Williamson speaks directly to this issue:

> Our deepest fear is not that we are inadequate. Our deepest fear is that we are powerful beyond measure. It is our light, not our darkness that most frightens us. We ask ourselves, 'Who am I to be brilliant, gorgeous, talented, fabulous?' Actually, who are you not to be? You are a child of God. Your playing small does not serve the world. There is nothing enlightened about shrinking so that other people won't feel insecure around you. We are all meant to shine, as children do. We were born to make manifest the glory of God that is within us. It's not just in some of us; it's in everyone. And as we let our own light shine, we unconsciously give other people permission to do the same. As we are liberated from our own fear, our presence automatically liberates others.[9]

"It" is an expression of the deepest, most authentic, parts of our self; "Our Soul's Jewelry," our God in form, our bad-ass true self stripped away from the nasty neural and cultural ruts that would have us believing otherwise. That's why those who have It seem larger-than-life. They are expressing themselves at a higher level than what is required for basic living. If you've got It, you are one step closer to giving godly experiences—or gifts of grace. In fact, in German, *gottheit*, means "deity" (essential nature of a god). "Gottheit" = "Got the It." Get it?

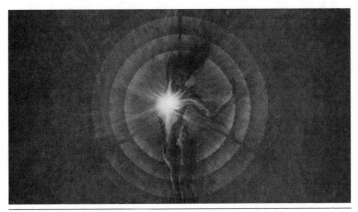

Gottheit by Martin Bridge

THE FIVE QUALITIES OF THE CONTAGIOUS PERSON

First, what is a contagious person? Contagious people are peeps who "Got the It." Contagious people spread memes like Aunt Jemima spreads syrup. These folks know how to *show their value.* Like the little teapot, they sing during their morning walks, "Tip me over and pour me out!" (Death metal versions, fine.) The contagious person is all in with life and therefore capable of being all out. Think Jimi Hendrix, Steve Jobs, and Ellen. The contagious person knows that, as Ms. Williamson says, "As they let their own light shine, they unconsciously give other people permission to do the same."[10] The result: Revolution.

I gravitate towards contagious people. Many of us do, because we generally feel good around them. As a charismologist, I've studied this particular animal with vigor, and I've found five qualities virtually every meme-making, extraordinary, contagious person seems to possess. Lucky for memory ease, the five make an acronym: PPECC, like a baby chicken PPECCs at its outgrown eggshell, so it can bust out and fly free.

"You know what truly aches all that you are? Having so much inside you and not having the slightest clue as to how to pour it out."

CHRISTOPHER POINDEXTER

First, there's **Presence:** You gotta be present to develop magnetic presence. Your presence is the ultimate present you give.* Want to practice building your presence right this instant? Here we go. *Listen* intently to everything that's going on inside you and around you. Your breath, the hum of the fridge, traffic. Don't judge or evaluate what you notice; simply observe.

Perseverance: When "they" tell you, no, ask again . . . and again. This has become a coaching cliché for a reason: You will not get the support you need for your revolution unless you persevere. They will throw tomatoes at you. Or simply ignore you. It's bound to happen. How you respond is the difference between the ordinary person and the extraordinary person. You will open doors that would otherwise be shut if you know in your gut that what you've got is going to make the world a better place. Choose to be great and then bank on your choice. As a great man once told me after a personal door-shutting-in-my-face experience, "Ahhh, Robin, the door shut on you but you kept knocking until it opened. You have discovered the grace that comes from perseverance and conviction. Well done."**

Execution: When you say you're going to do something, do it. Follow-through is mandatory for making a mark, building a team, and creating confidence. No one will stay in your superorganism if you can't be trusted to do the part you say you're going to do. Besides, how are you going to follow your dreams through to fruition if you don't execute them? Execution is the mark of a true revolutionary. Lots of people dream. Few make their dreams real. Do what you say you're going to do. Should something interfere with your follow-through, communicate with your team.

Also of note: Get it out there; don't wait till it's perfect. Trust the world in which you share yourself and your projects, and it will help you get to the next level. When I was writing *The Charisma Code,* I had no idea the United Nations would want

---

* Refer to Step One: Confidence, for presence-building activities.
** Thank you for this, Michael Levine.

to launch it at their headquarters and give a copy to every UN ambassador present. I didn't have any connections at the UN before I wrote this book. It was only because I put my manuscript out there before it was perfect and published, that the world could contribute to my book's success in ways I could not do alone. In sum: don't hide; do what you say you're going to do; and let the world contribute. In biz terms: test your market and let your market change you and your product.

Courage: I've got special affection for Genghis Khan, the notorious conqueror. If he were with us today, here's what I imagine Khan would say: "Robin, I'm enjoying *The Charisma Code,* but you should be more aggressive in encouraging people to let their charisma out. They're afraid it will be like stripping in front of a prim and proper audience. They think they're going to be shunned and laughed at. Without the courage to risk making a stinking fool of themselves, they won't discover that the opposite occurs."

Thanks, GK. It's true. Letting your charisma shine is the gift of grace that "automatically liberates others." Thing is, you may need more courage than you think you're going to need to repeatedly show your self to a world that has barely started to love its own big bad self. Begin practicing today. Take baby steps. Continue by doing something that scares you every day. The world responds to fearlessness. Do not shy away from *who you are.*

Compassion: Our fifth and final quality, compassion, may be the most overlooked of them all. Our culture values **Courageous** super heroes on the silver screen, because they embody **Presence,** they **Persevere,** and they **Execute** (traditionally while kicking literal butt). We love quantifiable, visible action. The challenge is that compassion is often invisible. However, its subtle power is undeniable and necessary. Speaking its own language beyond words, compassion helps everyone and everything. As such, people ache to be near it. It also brings the five qualities of the contagious person into full-circle PPECC, as

Compassion requires surrender to the first quality, **Presence.**
Everything is perfect just as it is.

GAZE INTO YOUR DEMONS

Everything is perfect just as it is.

The Western bias against self-love is not universal. In ancient India, folks interpreted one's falling in love with one's own reflection in a much different way. There, they esteemed (and in many places still do) the tantric practice of mirror gazing. To mirror gaze, you simply look into your own eyes . . . deeply, deeply . . . letting your eyes soften . . . releasing your focus . . . gazing beyond facial lines or tight or loose jowls . . . beyond the color of your eyes . . . beyond the pigment specks . . . into . . . you.

I have an invitation for you: Make an appointment with your mirror and go have a gaze. If you do, however, remember this: Seeing who you really are is not for the faint of heart, but, as is written into the storyline of every great quest, the hero must meet his monsters to gain access to the gates of liberation. Moving past the monster at the gate is the key to finding the treasure she or he has spent a whole life seeking. No one gets to walk through without this confrontation; no one gets charisma without knowing they are made of great stuff; and the only way to know is to confront your monsters. So keep gazing, and, if you meet your monsters, know that you are standing in front of your gates of liberation. Your treasure is near. Keep gazing—stay in the game. You can only win.

When you find the Great, within you or someone else, you feel compelled to follow it, trust it, froth at the bit for more of it. Charismatics making use of their soul-bred authority make us want to believe in them. They speak to us in a language beyond words, beyond the rational. They use the same letters and sounds as everyone else, but in the hands of a charismatic, somehow those letters and sounds are like custom-made arrows on an archetypal bow, cocked back in soulful conviction. Charismatics pull back that bow, aim, and fire, tearing us open with a passion born of the conviction they have something they *must* share, and we let them. Because, gag if you will, each human craves to be in the presence of an authority that has our best, most awake interest at heart. We pretend we want to be in control, but most of us secretly ache to be led.

We flock to charismatics like Oprah to have our heartstrings strummed. We watch Charlie Chaplin to help us laugh our worries away. We are drawn to the speeches of John F. Kennedy and Martin Luther King, Jr. so that we may live their passion and perspective. Charismatics make us feel the magnitude of what our human form is capable of. We want to be saved from our own little thinking and timid heartbeats. If humans are wired to benefit so much from charismatic individuals, then it must be a pretty important evolutionary trait. And you have it! Start by taking your self out of hiding.

Disclaimer: We are not perfect. Even as charismatics, we miss the bullseye sometimes. We fall off. We disconnect. Sometimes we hurt millions. Mostly, we fall off in little ways. We overeat or lose our temper with people we love. We arrive late for work or forget an important date. The trick is to not take yourself so seriously that you lose your confidence and presence. This is the literal meaning of "sin," and we are all sinful. In its original Hebrew and Greek, "sin" simply means "to miss the mark." It's an archery term. Life is not a dress rehearsal, but it is a game. Pick up your bow and take your best shot. If you miss your target, simply pick up another arrow and shoot again.

CONCLUSION

Rebelling against self-repression is not just a gift to yourself, it's an example to others. It's a way to give everyone around you permission to radiate their God-given light with the intensity of the sun. Plus, hiding your brilliance isn't attractive. It's dull, and what fun is that? If someone around you is dull, you can still shine. If people are arrogant or selfish with you, you can have compassion, because selfishness is not malicious. It comes from a lack of self-acceptance. They don't feel they're good enough to share themselves with you. However, if you shine, you give them permission, and once selfish people let greatness crumble their walls, they don't choose selfishness anymore.

I once heard Dr. Jean Houston, the revered human potential expert and social activist, say that a human being's greatest potential is accessed when they empower others. Indeed, loving ourselves is the first ray of power everyone needs to sprout into a great flower. That liberated narcissist's full bloom can go on to empower others. When we know we're made of great stuff, we show ourselves—it's that simple.

Let's rewrite myths together. Let's fly to the sun and learn how the sun makes light, so we can give it to the people. (It's just a hunch, but I don't think the gods will punish us.)

In the next section, I'll talk about the power of mimicry. As you dare to rebel against actions that are no longer true for you, you'll find a big question mark looming:

What do I do instead?

Luckily, the world is full of ideas! Once you know you are worthy of mimicking Greatness, doing it is a piece of cake.

2. SECOND HALF: GROWING YOUR SELF INTO A GOD

After the fourth century CE, the word "charisma" all but disappeared. Charismatic Christianity still used it, but it was as esoteric to the mainstream as alchemical words like "nigredo" and "albedo"* (You know those, right? Right.) Then, in 1922, German sociologist Max Weber gave us this definition:

---

* In alchemical terms, "nigredo" and "albedo" are two of the three primary stages base metals transition through on their journey towards refinement into gold.

Charisma is a certain quality of an individual personality by virtue of which he is set apart from ordinary men and treated as endowed with supernatural, superhuman, or at least specifically exceptional powers or qualities. These are such as are not accessible to the ordinary person, but are regarded as of divine origin or as exemplary, and on the basis of them, the individual concerned is treated as a leader.[11]

Weber's definition caught like wildfire, putting the word "charisma" into our modern lexicon for the first time. Indeed, his definition is still the way most of us think of charisma. But Weber's definition was highly criticized. He never told us what the "supernatural powers" were. He just called them "exemplary" and told us such people are "set apart from ordinary men." This view explains why most of us think charisma cannot be learned and that charismatic individuals are born with powers "not accessible to the ordinary person." With all due respect to Mr. Weber, this is a load of baloney.

There is no denying that some people are currently charismatic, while others are not—yet. But to think it has to be that way is scientifically impossible! As author and entrepreneur Seth Godin said in a recent blog,

You can learn math. French. Bowling. You can learn Javascript, too. But you can also learn to be more empathetic, passionate, focused, consistent, persistent and twenty-seven other attitudes. If you can learn to be better at something, it's a skill. And if it's a skill, it's yours if you want it. Which is great news, isn't it?[12]

Yes, Seth, it's absolutely great news. So here's how to be skillfully charismatic: Any kind of human behavior, from using a toilet to singing opera, emerges through a combination of introspective question-asking and mimicry. Obviously when one unique person mimics the actions of another unique person, the results will differ. But it's a branching pattern. That's basically how things get learned in this species of ours, and charisma is no different.

Have you ever noticed that dogs look like their owners and old couples look like each other? Our mimicking behavior affects not only our looks. Studies show a person's income is typically the median of that of the five people they spend the most time with.[13] Our emotional climate is also affected: Research by Nicholas Christakis of Harvard Medical School and James Fowler of the University of California, San Diego, shows that when an individual becomes happy, a friend living within a mile experiences a 25 percent increased chance of becoming happy too. For the neighbors next door, that cheering probability rises to 34 percent.[14] People even look like the cities they live in (bear with me here). In my early twenties, I often traveled between homes in Las Vegas and Hawaii. In Las Vegas I was always ten pounds slimmer than when I lived in Hawaii. My Vegas body was cut with an aggressive edge to survive, like everything in that desert environment. In Hawaii, my curves grew with a quality that matched the lush tropical landscape.

You become what you relate to and what you relate with. As cited in the research above, this includes moods and emotional states. If you respond to anger with anger, you become an angry person. Respond to joy with joy, and you become joyful. Enact revenge on someone, and you become revenge. Show compassion towards someone, and you become compassion. Your physiology requires that you become a vessel for everything you serve up. Coffee doesn't leave the pot without leaving its color and temperature behind on the porcelain.

Many psychologists specialize in treating actors after they finish a movie or play. A good actor relates to and with his character so intimately that he gets "stained" with that character's qualities. You can imagine what that could do to your home life if you're constantly cast as the villain, or the banker with suicidal tendencies, or worse.

However, you have a choice. A neuroscientist will say you become what you repeatedly pay attention to. A charismologist will say you become what you repeatedly relate to. Pay your attention first, so you can relate second, because attention grants access to relationship. Question: If you become what you relate to, what you pay attention to, to whom and to what will you pay *your* attention?

Choose wisely.

There's a whole world, within and without, wanting your attention. You have virtually unlimited options: public figures, historical figures, fictional figures, deities, your mom, your grandpa, your thoughts that love you, and your thoughts that don't—just to name a few. As you select your sources to attend to, relate to, and mimic, I invite you to think outside your own culture. While the West doesn't encourage self-love, the West is not the world. When I visited with people in Kenyan villages, I was fascinated with the way they walked; they had a low center of gravity and loose hips. Their postures were noticeably straight and aligned, heads stacked directly above hips, a posture that also served their utilitarian need to carry heavy baskets on their heads with skill and grace.

This alignment spoke to me in nonverbal charisma code. It told me these people were inhabiting the moment: *Yes, I love being in this body; I am right where I want to be.* In contrast, if you go to any Western, industrialized city, you will see people speeding this way and that, their top halves slanting forward as if they are not yet where they are supposed to be; their heads are moving fast, but their bodies can't keep up. This way of carrying oneself creates an enormous sense of incongruence, incoherence, and discontentment. It is nonverbal charisma code for physical disharmony between mind and body.

The more connected you are to a particular culture, the more you will unknowingly act out that culture's norms, including the way you walk. By redirecting your attention, you can counter these non-It forces. Here's an idea: Have someone take a movie of you walking, then look at it together. What does it reveal about you and the culture you identify with?

I didn't grow up with the kind of singing, dancing, and merrymaking practiced by "tribes" that value It. My best friend did, though. So I spent most Sundays with Tynesia and her big family, eating soul feasts and boogying to Michael Jackson.

At a young age, I learned I also loved roller coasters and being tossed upside down by my father. Although my birth tribe didn't value the embodiment of It the way some other world tribes do, I was drawn to joy and surrender like an insect to a bit of light.

Dancing was made of the same squealing fabric as my roller coaster. I turned on my mimicking ability and danced my holy It into being with my Sunday family. Soon, I was an honorary member of Tynesia's tribe. By choosing to relate to joy and liveliness, I became a part of a joyful, lively community. My particular niche was dancing, but charismatic interaction can happen in any setting, from playing Parcheesi with old folks to constructing the ultimate ad campaign. *What will your niche be?*

Can you see the puzzle coming together? Charisma is not, as Weber proposed, a special quality that an individual is born with. Rather, each individual is culturally influenced by their "tribe" to have It or not. If you were born into a tribe that glorified and esteemed It, then you learned that collecting and expressing It is an important part of relating. In many tribes, having It versus not having It can make the difference between getting affection or food or starving for both. If that was the case, you probably went out and got It!

Depending on your birth-tribe's dynamics, you learned quickly which behaviors to mimic to get that affection and food. It may be that they didn't encourage It-like qualities. If so, you probably learned to mimic their deflection. Hence, you are reading this book and will go on to find a new tribe. Good choice!

Once you decide to become great, you must decide what sort of great you want to be. Unfortunately, Weber's definition has had us believing for nearly a century that charisma is a finite resource, but remember, like many of us, Weber was the product of a deeply secular and disenchanted society. Although his charisma was different from Paul's, there is a common thread of truth between the two: *Charisma is a gift that grants special powers to those who have it.*

HOW TO GET SPECIAL POWERS

It don't mean a thing if it ain't got that swing.

ELLA FITZGERALD

Become aware of whom you are mimicking when you walk, sit, and stand. There is flesh made of blood cells and muscle fibers, and then there is flesh that uses its blood cells and muscle fibers to tell an engaging story. Think about a dancing sex icon's coveted curve of thigh. Now think of that same thigh in the morgue. See the difference? It ain't the leg, baby.

Just as you started getting in the moment by paying attention to food, start selecting for greatness by noticing your physicality. Pay attention to what your body is mimicking. Are you slouching (relating to exhaustion), or sitting on the counter (relating to chopping boards)? Do you sit like a king or a sex kitten? Are your arms crossed in self-protection or loose and ready to hug?

Research from social psychologist Amy Cuddy shows that "high-power poses" (think Wonder Woman's posture) versus "low-power poses" (Homer Simpson) affect not only the way others perceive us. They affect our personal body chemistry. Any time you take up space, open up, assume positions of fearlessness, celebration, and victory, your testosterone (dominance hormone) increases while your cortisol (stress hormone) goes down. Wonder-Womanesque victory poses grant you the testy courage to be dominant in expression and likely to handle high-stress situations without freaking out. Here are the facts:

After only two minutes in a high-power pose, subjects in Cuddy's research experienced a whopping 20 percent increase in testosterone and a 25 percent decrease in cortisol! Similarly, after two minutes in a low-power pose, subjects experienced a 10 percent decrease in testosterone and a 15 percent increase in cortisol.[15] FYI: Research suggests that most great leaders, either female or male, have higher than "normal" testosterone levels and lower than "normal" cortisol levels. In light of Cuddy's discoveries, I'm considering taking my executive clients to Comic-Con animation conventions dressed up as Superman and Batwoman.

In sum: All it takes is two minutes of assuming the position of "I'm grand" to get your body chemistry on board with your declaration. Want to try "I'm grand" on for size? Raise your arms into a *V* above your head, widen your stance, and let your face adopt an expression congruent with this new posture for two minutes. Practice regularly at home. The next time you are getting out of your car to attend a meeting, tell yourself that when your foot touches the pavement you will instantaneously assume a posture of confidence and victory. Open up. Take up space. You may even smile contentedly to yourself as you experience the quiet joy of knowing the value of the gifts you are about to let loose on the meeting. Remember one of the basic premises of this book is to know, without doubt, that you bring value to every situation.

Want to add even more value to your interactions at your next meeting? Touch is one way you can significantly affect the hormones of someone else! So let's say you assume a victory pose for a couple minutes, thus lowering your cortisol and increasing your testosterone—you're feeling goooood. On the way to your meeting you ask yourself, *what if I present so clearly and with such conviction with CISCO's VP that she decides to produce all future routers using our new technology?* With a naturally emerging smile, you open the door to the conference room at CISCO, shake the VP's hand and begin your presentation. It goes well. They ask questions; you answer. On your way out the door, you naturally and gently touch the VP on her shoulder as you bend down to pick up your briefcase, which is on the floor beside her chair. It was a simple touch that carried a dual function of letting her know you were there so she didn't accidently step on you while picking up your bag, as well as fulfilling your purpose to connect using a powerful language beyond words in as many ways as possible. You succeeded. It turns out that touch releases a feel-good, trust-establishing hormone called oxytocin, while reducing the stress hormone cortisol, which you lowered in yourself earlier while assuming a victory pose.

Touch increases the likelihood that people will do what you request. Check out the research: Studies reveal that students who receive touch from their teacher are nearly twice as likely to volunteer in class as those who are not touched. And get this: Waiters who gave their customers a light touch on the shoulder while presenting the bill were shown to have a tip increase from 11.5 percent up to 14.9 percent![16]

Certainly different cultures around the world interpret touch differently—as do varied environments within one country. Some individuals, often due to past trauma, do not want to be touched. With that said, touch is a universal language beyond words that produces oxytocin and diminishes cortisol—regardless of culture. Use your best judgment, and remember touch keeps releasing all those feel-good hormones you got moving in yourself during your victory pose and positive use of your whatiferousness superpower. Touch results in the strengthening of social bonds, trust, and a greater propensity to collaborate.

One trinity of actions you can take, should you wish to:

A) Assume a posture that shows you know your value;

B) Show your value by confidently using touch to communicate your trustworthiness, goodwill, and desire to connect and;

C) Make room for inspiration.

MAKING ROOM FOR INSPIRATION

Our bodies rebel against tedious, boring tasks by cramping, slouching, and aching. They feel good when we creatively engage with things we love, so let yourself be drawn into what you love and watch as your posture changes. Have you ever seen a person you considered to be charismatic who didn't seem to want to be where they were, with those they were with, and doing what they were doing? Exactly.

One way to make room for inspiration is to empty your hardworking head. You can leave the straight thoughts of your noggin when they begin to weigh you down with the monotonous mundane by simply shaking your head around while engaging in an activity that increases your pulse and oxygen intake. Wobble said head and you won't be able to keep a straight thought. I'm serious! Turn your spin class into a trance class by closing your eyes and rocking out with your head in a rhythmic pattern while spinning dem fine leggies of yours. Sometimes you simply need to leave yourself to come back with more of yourself. Practice the tried-and-true ways of our global indigenous ancestors by electing to engage in ordeals and regular rhythmic head-shaking mini-trances. Best not to have to depend on intoxicants to relieve you from the tedious. If you are truly interested in cultivating long-standing charisma, you will need to learn to enter the numinous in between the business of a full day.

GODS CREATE

One night, while writing, I looked down at my typing hands and saw lines and veins of time, etched in a way that only my living biology could striate. It struck me then: I did not have an ounce of disgust for them. Instead, my eyes welled at the beauty of my hands, as rare and precious now as they were yesterday and as they will be tomorrow. The French speak about this more than most: as your body grows older through joyful tasks, you will only become more beautiful.

You get special powers by selectively relating with things that give you power. That's why *The Charisma Code* guides you to love yourself first before guiding you consciously to grow yourself into a god. When you love yourself, you relate with people, places, things, and emotions that encourage you to experience your value. You are then more likely to respond to life as a creator, using your self-made authority to generate valuable, culture-enhancing contributions.

You were born a god. Gods create.

Creation is simply making something out of nothing. When you pump out a thought, where did it come from? How about when you splatter a puddle of rain. How did it happen? And when you ask, *"What if?"* what's going on *there*? *Something out of nothing. Hmm . . . this is sounding quite a bit like the big bang!*

In all seriousness, the value of your creations is a reflection of how much you value yourself. You are using your god-creativity powers with every new ingredient you plop into our soup. Every time you make a creation, every time you make something out of nothing, ask a question, think a thought, speak a word, assume a pose, paint a picture, give a kiss, avoid a kiss—you *show your value*.

Let's examine two contrasting examples of charisma and see what we can learn. First, we have Madonna. Madonna, like Mary Pickford, is a spectacular woman who's undoubtedly GotTheIt. In the beginning of her career, she was a bit shy on vocal talent, but she didn't let that stop her, and let's face it: When we imagine Madonna, vocal prowess is not the first thing that springs to mind. Rather, we imagine pointy bras, vogue hand gestures, gyrating diamonds on a tight body, and . . . It. Madonna has been able to sustain connection with her fan base for decades. If we wanted to reverse-engineer Madonna, here are two things we might examine:

- **MADONNA IS BOLD.** That woman is unafraid to pull her soul's jewelry out of the closet and glorify environments with It. She puts her magnificence out there, and we can't help but feel magnetized by her display. She obviously loves to take her audience for a ride on "Madonna: The Force of Nature." With that said, not everyone likes her. From the get-go she was getting major flack from Catholics, who said her performances were devil-sent, and from liberated women, who said she was sending them back to the Dark Ages; but, as successful artists know, "No press is bad press." I will add to that: "No press is bad press as long as you believe you are dishing out great stuff." If you doubt what you are offering, the bad publicity will fulfill your secret I'm-bad-stuff belief. Once you think you are bad stuff, you will probably evacuate the premises. Goodbye career in the limelight. So, should you ever be faced with "bad press," *stop*. Get still; and remember your value.

- **MADONNA IS AN INNOVATOR.** After her career bloomed in the 80's, she didn't stop; she surrendered each successful hit and kept recreating herself to the pulse of each new generation. She demonstrated an uncanny ability to listen to the times and respond to them; or, maybe she was such a strong cultural meme creator, it was we who reshaped our culture in response to her lead. Madonna can never be accused of being stagnant. She stretches her *Homo sapiens* innovation power to the max.

So let's say you're new to a country. You might be an immigrant or a refugee or just want a new life in a new place; how can you mimic Madonna's innovative boldness to help yourself find belonging in your new country? First, you can recognize that the great stuff you bring to a place is the differences you bring to it. When you bring new values, customs, and ways of relating to a country used to doing things "just so," you offer an opportunity for that country to be affected by the memes you bring. So let's imagine you fled from Syria and are beginning to make a new home in Germany. Your ability to contribute your unique dances, food, poetry, dress, family focus, and inclination to better your life offers Germans an opportunity to integrate your flavor into their country's stew. There will be certain traits very few Germans will take in and take on; those traits will not influence much of Germany's stew flavor. But know this: your presence will keep Germany's culture fresh and innovative if they choose to relate with you!

All good things come to an end when they stop innovating their systems to reflect the current demands of their environments. Look at Rome or any once-powerful empire, such as the Hapsburgs or the colonial British, that crumbled under the weight of what eventually became false power. Power becomes false when it stops dialoguing with what it is there to serve. Fallen empires almost always fall under the rule of men who try to will their fantasy into reality instead of responding to and dialoguing with reality. These leaders, under the delusion of their own hubris and fear, seem to think that if their rule worked once, it will keep working no matter what changes around them. That's like fantasizing that wildlife sanctuaries will stay the same once you build a massive super highway through them.

Remember biomimicry, the process of mimicking nature's genius for human inventions? We've discussed the way that, in nature, life creates conditions conducive to the flourishing of life. Here's another 3.8-billion-year-old life principle that you can see everywhere: nature is locally attuned and responsive. This means that thriving organisms on planet Earth do not exist in isolation. Instead, they adapt their behaviors and survival mechanisms to accommodate and relate with what's going on around them. Leaders that would rather not look at the sociopolitical and spiritual changes occurring around them will end up hurting themselves and the people they lead.

In contrast, let's look at Madonna's life as well as the technology supergiant Facebook; here we see innovation as one of the primary fuels of their success. Their bold move to *show their value* while bringing their creativity to the masses through their constant innovations is what brought them to the top and, for the most part, kept them there. But Madonna and Facebook are locally attuned and responsive to their customers as well. If a strategy, song, or web interface is not working for the people they are serving, they listen and move on to their next innovation. Change is good. As the Buddha says, "Change is the only thing we can depend on; it is the only constant." So back to imagining you're a Syrian refugee. If you boldly offer your unique cultural gifts to Germany and they intelligently receive them into the broth of their current culture, your diverse addition will create an innovative environment that is likely to not only boost Germany's global flavor but also increase their gross domestic product. Falafel and fattoush anybody?

Now let's address a very dark example and learn from it: Adolf Hitler. Hitler did have charisma, and Hitler used the currency of connection. However, he also used the currency of separation. That's obvious. For educational reasons, let us investigate how he used the currency of connection.

Hitler's success at amassing an enormous following in Nazi Germany was due in part to his ability to play on humanity's superorganism nature. As collaborative human creatures, we long to play our part. We crave belonging.

The gift that Hitler gave his followers at rallies like the annual Nazi Party Congress in Nuremberg was to create an overwhelming sense of group identity. When he spoke, individual soldiers were no longer scared, separate organisms trying to survive the Great Depression. As a group, they had a specific superorganism function to perform. They were needed. They belonged to something. As part of the larger group, their smallness dissolved into the group's greater purpose. William Shirer describes this phenomenon in his *Berlin Diary*:

> [T]here, in the floodlit night, [the congress-goers] achieved the highest state of being the Germanic man knows: the shedding of their individual souls and minds . . . until under the mystic lights and at the sound of the magic words of the Austrian they were merged completely in the German herd.[17]

Adolph Hitler used his currency of connection to do what charisma does best: impregnate others with a feeling of the Great. He did what all great leaders do. He brought the tribe together and created a functioning superorganism. The Nazis' downfall came not from spending their connection currency but from the nature of their shared goal. The process Hitler employed to create national identity and belonging for the "German herd" included the persecution, torture, and murder of eleven million living, breathing, dreaming humans. Because this was essentially a parasitic-cheater strategy, it had a massive price to pay. Namely, the ecosystem of the larger group (the world) was brought wrongly out of balance and naturally fought back. Hitler did not create conditions conducive to the flourishing of life and Hitler was not locally attuned and responsive to the world. Hitler and all of Nazi Germany lost the war miserably.

Hitler's misuse of power raises the question: What brings about the desire to spend the currency of separation? How is it that any group can enact racial genocide on another? Answer:

They must first lose the ability to see the sentient value in the "other." At the time of the Holocaust, one of the derogatory terms the Nazis used to refer to the Jews was "food wasters." As the Dalai Lama puts it in his classic, *Ethics for the New Millennium:*

> Events such as those which occurred at Auschwitz are violent reminders of what can happen when individuals—and by extension, whole societies—lose touch with basic human feeling.

What can we learn from Hitler?

- The currency of connection fulfills our human need to be part of something larger.

- Not all "larger somethings" are beneficial.

- The nature of the superorganism's shared purpose is paramount. The currency of connection can be used towards any goal, ethical or otherwise.

- An unethical goal will have a hefty price tag. Using separation currency creates enemies. Energy allocated towards defense instead of revolutionary progress will not get you anywhere.

- A sustainable charismatic movement gets its legs from gifting the replenishing power of empowerment by including others' value—not excluding it.

Although this tale may sound cautionary, if you follow *The Charisma Code* teachings, you will perpetuate only empowering revolutionary memes. This is because, when we cultivate our connection with our greatest self, know our real value, and relate in each moment with an eye for value, we can't help but cultivate empathy for all whom we encounter. We become what we relate with and protect what we feel connected to, and all of this happens in the present, *now*. Jewish folks have a word connecting It to now: *itster*, meaning "now" in Yiddish. Moved by the aliveness we find in our environment, an Itster can't help but feel, so look for the It in every now, and you will learn to *feel*.

Let's inspect our English dictionary for the current cultural norm surrounding the word "it":

Merriam Webster defines "it" as "that one—usually in reference to a lifeless thing." Indeed, "it" has been chosen by the populous as a way to curtly reference things, inanimate objects. It's easy to talk about the plastic cup as an "it," or the business card, or her nose; but what would happen if we recognized and related with the aliveness in every "it" we encounter? What if we saw the life force in that broccoli floweret? How about the photon energy radiating from our bedside lamp, doing its level best to mimic the sun, declaring the genius of Nikola Tesla and Thomas Edison?

Hitler's mishaps loudly declare the need to extend our feelers and compassion to groups we do not inherently belong to. We have a biological imperative to nurture our gene pool and the groups we feel are responsible for our survival, but what if we sought to find our interconnectedness with groups we do not identify with? What if we went so far as to investigate how we might be interconnected with our enemies? Or to wild wolves? Or the ocean?

As it says in the Qur'an, "We have created you male and female, and have made you nations and tribes that ye may know one another."[18] Use your powers of authority and influence ethically by seeking to "know one another."

DEEPER INTO THE DARK SIDE

Many of us soft humans choose not to "know one another." We spend much of our time in a quandary, wondering if we can trust the charming, the influential, and the magnetic. We crimp up, wondering if people are busy orchestrating a way to hurt us. We wonder if the seemingly charismatic pursuer or church leader or political party president is trustworthy. We wonder about others so much that we begin to wonder about ourselves.

To avoid such debilitating thought patterns, let's break down the currencies a bit more. Here are some fast ways to quickly read what currency is in prominent use during any given situation:

Separation currency uses "us *against* them" strategies to make people feel like they are connected to a tribe and a purpose. Phrases like "they threaten us" are used to identify an enemy in order to motivate group collaboration. Spenders of separation currency have not done their human homework on seeing others' value.

Connection currency uses "us *with* them" strategies to establish ever-widening networks and energy-enhancing ripples of connection. Phrases like "they add to us" are used to establish allies and grow group collaboration possibilities. All spenders of connection currency have passed the exam on seeing others' value.

These currencies aren't just a way to separate cult leaders from leaders worthy of your follow. You spend one of these two currencies every time you *show your self*. In other words, you exude either separation or connection currency each time you risk putting yourself out there. Are you against certain people but with others?

Charisma helps you connect. It helps inspire people to jump onboard your ship towards a common goal. Charisma propels you to make a mark. Make something happen with your charisma and you will feel significant. The need for significance is responsible for the creation of both philanthropists and killers.

Days before Christopher Harper Mercer gunned down nine students and himself at Umpqua Community College in Oregon, he was reported to have commented on "Kickass Torrents," an online blog, about Vester Flanagan, the gunman who killed two US journalists live on air in August 2015. Mercer's comment read, Vester "got his face splashed across every screen, his name across the lips of every person on the planet"[19] after murdering former colleagues live, on air, the previous month. Significant?

The data compiled by the crowd-sourced site Mass Shooting Tracker reveals an even more shocking human toll: in the United States, there is a mass shooting—defined as four or more people shot in one incident—nearly every day.

Why is this happening? Regardless of laws around weapon availability, the fact is in the United States people are killing large numbers of innocent people at an alarmingly elevated rate. I think we can all agree that this is not a cultural meme we want to continue to spread. So I'll ask again, why is this happening? Are the killers sane? I'm not sure you can be a killer and be sane. So no, they're not. But then we must ask what makes these killers perform their insane acts of separation? Might the desire to be in the limelight, in the media, making a significant impact on a world that never understood them be part of the reason? I believe it is.

These dark examples of spending separation currency are tantrum cries for connection currency. They are violent reminders that we all need to be "seen."

What can we learn from these bloody examples?

1) **Know your value** and your creations will reflect that value. Remember: Who you are is before the "word." Before what they said about you or didn't say. Before what they saw in you or didn't see. You are more powerful than the peanut gallery.

2) **See others' value** and maybe, just maybe, you will be one of the angels that help turn a potential killer into a person who feels calmly significant.

Power is a neutral force. Bullets shot into bodies exclaim power. True charisma is a very specific type of power; it is the power of grace. Grace occurs at the intersection between separation and connection. Grace happens when what once was lost now is found. Inclusion invites a place for grace.

ON GROWING SMARTER

"Seeking to know one another" may not only help put an end to the shocking regularity of mass shootings; it will also help you get smarter. Here's the science: The more diversity we expose ourselves to, the more we increase the synaptic connections in our brains. Our synaptic connections tell us what's possible, make us better problem solvers and turn us into more creative contributors at work and in bed. In other words, the more synaptic connections you've got goin' on in that skull of yours, the larger your paint box of "colors" to change the world.

Want to inspire truly fresh innovations in your business? Hire a diverse team. Want to create yourself anew? Relate with the new. You become what you relate to.

THE GLOBAL CITIZEN

You know what I want to create with my godly powers?

More than understanding the biological constituents of dirt so I can prepare mixtures of new and improved, pristine dirt—more than learning the real estate market so I can invest in good homes that make me lots of money—more than making babies, I want to contribute to the emerging culture of the global citizen.

Sound lofty? It ain't. Globally, technology bonds us as much as the threat of climate change; what happens to the dollar affects the value of the Chinese *renminbi*; global outrage over the treatment of women affects Indian legislation; and on and on and on. The era of global citizenship is here. The next big innovations will spring from global culture. They must. The global citizen is a very real entity. Her kingdom does not stop at her white picket fence, her neighborhood's gate, or her country's barbed wire. Her kingdom is the whole wide planet. One of the great personal gifts that come with honing this planetary perspective is that *a global citizen feels at home wherever she goes.* How does she do that? She looks with playful curiosity at the differences she encounters. She may even try on and mimic "odd" behaviors, thus enhancing her dynamic presence. She playfully, curiously, and with wonder seeks to understand instead of judge. In other words, quoting the Qur'an once more, global citizens seek to "know one another."

The result? A culture of peace.

A CULTURE OF PEACE
Peace efforts will continually fail until people embrace humanity's oneness.
AMBASSADOR ANWARUL K. CHOWDHURY
FORMER UNDER-SECRETARY-GENERAL
AND HIGH REPRESENTATIVE OF THE U.N.

WHAT WILL YOU CREATE?

CREATE YOUR REVOLUTION
What follows is a practical path to creating revolution:
1. **Disruption**
2. **Innovation**
3. **Revolution**

DISRUPTION
What do you do when you notice something not working?

You stop doing the thing that's not working. You disrupt the broken pattern! For example, when researchers discovered that mercury fillings caused severe health problems for some people, many dentists stopped using mercury in their fillings.

INNOVATION
Once you identify the broken system, it's time to innovate!

As long as there are human mouths, there will be a need for fillings.

Many dentists have switched from mercury to gold, porcelain, or composite resin fillings. Mercury (or silver amalgam) fillings are still used in many places, but the "revolution" towards nonmercury fillings is well under way.

REVOLUTION

Originally, your innovation (this includes your culturally "odd" behaviors if you're new to a country or neighborhood or office) may be mocked and given little credibility or attention. Then once it gains traction, there will be those who resist and fight the change you bring. If your innovation is truly good, it will eventually become the new normal.

Although some consider concern around mercury fillings to be quackery, alternative fillings are popping up everywhere.

THE PATH OF LEAST RESISTANCE

You never change things by fighting the existing reality.
To change something, build a new model
that makes the existing model obsolete.

BUCKMINSTER FULLER

Fearful resistance from the old guard is the most frustrating thing you will encounter as you bring your innovation to society. What to do? Well, you can fight it, protest it and talk s——t about it. Or . . . you can save lots of time and strife by taking the path of least resistance.

Let's pretend you're deeply passionate about innovative dentistry, but the big guys invested in the old way start thwarting you with court cases and break-ins. Your path of least resistance might look like starting your cutting-edge holistic dental clinic in a more alternative-friendly part of the world. Believers in your work may travel thousands of miles to receive your treatment.

They will tell their friends, post on social media, and start a buzz. If your treatment works, your holistic dentistry methods will hit a tipping point and take on a life of their own. Then, your job is to step out of the way. Lasting revolutions occur when you let your followers lead.

THE HERO

Be warned, when you leave the mainstream to find better ways, even with the noblest of intentions to take the path of least resistance as you bring back the goods from the mainstream's tributaries as a means to contribute to culture, you will still run into challenges. There are rarely the systems in place to socially and therefore economically support your innovation. Being tested in this way will challenge your tenacity as well as your belief in yourself and the new way you bring. This is a warning, yes. But not to worry; this is simply the hero's journey at play. The challenge is what will fortify you. Should you allow yourself to be made by the trials of integrating your innovation into mainstream culture, you will experience the life of the Greats as it pumps through your blood. The pain is worth it. Stay with it and you will be made a hero.

THE REBEL

Everything can be taken away from a man but one thing: the last of human freedoms—to choose one's attitude in any given set of circumstances.
DR. VICTOR FRANKL, NEUROLOGIST, PSYCHIATRIST, HOLOCAUST SURVIVOR

Let's do a quick recap: Becoming magnetic requires self-love, which allows us to feel worthy of becoming our own personal authority, a rebel. As a rebel, we begin to reflect on what alternatives we wish to bring to the world. From this seat of empowerment, we use our godly creative powers to dream up new ways of being, as well as to purposefully select the qualities in others we wish to reverse-engineer for ourselves. By learning from the trial and error of others, we can effectively spawn and foster the memes of our choosing. This feels wonderful! But beyond personal gain, there is a broader reason to cultivate magnetism: it's that changing-the-world thing. To prepare you for the next chapter, let's take a moment to talk about changing the world.

Dr. Mario Martinez tells a story about a psychological research experiment he calls "The Pioneer Fly." In the experiment, scientists set up a jar with flies in it, then covered the top of the jar. At first, the flies hit the sides of the glass, buzzing all around, frantically trying to get out. The surprise came when the scientists removed the lid a couple of days later, allowing the flies to move freely out of the jar. They did not fly out![20]

Dr. Ellen J. Langer from Harvard calls this phenomenon "premature cognitive commitment." PCC happens in all animals, from flies to rabbits to humans. When enough people (or one influential person) say, "That's just the way things are," we give up trying to see if things can be any other way.

Here's the coolness: When the scientists removed the lid, not all of the flies stayed in the jar. A few broke free from the "cognitive commitment" the other flies had made. Those free-flying, cultural-rebel buggers are known as the pioneer flies.

We all want out of the jar. Show us the way out.

Because we humans evolve quickly through mimicry, and because the vast percentage of our available examples in the West are of people living lives they do not love, most of us do not even think there is a way out. Despite our resources, despite our vast wealth, and because of a faulty belief that charisma is possessed only by a select few, we do not think to mimic those who have it. Many watch fabulous It folk on television but fall short of mimicking anything more than their Gucci bags, haircuts, and slang. However, by doing the work—by becoming a pioneer fly— you are literally embodying a much-needed example for those around you. You can bring the dead back to life.

Historically, Jesus is considered to be the first charismatic. If you remember Paul's definition of "charisma" as a gift of God's grace, it makes sense. Jesus was so full of Spirit and grace he couldn't help but gift It everywhere he went. He was also a pioneer fly. He overturned the money changers' tables at the temple and spoke about how powerful we all are. People flocked to him to have their suffering and ills relieved. He was magic, they said, a divine alchemist. He could transform water into wine. He could bring the dead back to life. What was his response? "These things and more shall you also do."[21] Be a Pioneer Fly. Set a divine example. Choose to *show your value.*

ONE MORE EXAMPLE

I once saw an eagle chained to a log. He was being shown by a bird-of-prey organization in front of a hundred kids and their parents. The owner of the organization apologized for the crying eagle. The eagle, chained to the log, wasn't crying; he was screaming. Every twenty seconds or so, he would try to fly. He flapped the biggest wings I had ever seen, screaming with their movement. He would "fly," full force, for four feet, demonstrating the grace and power he was made of, until the violence of the chain pulled him to the ground. The audience took pictures. I joined him in falling down.

It does not matter if someone chains you or you chain yourself. There is no greater indignity to the Source of Life than holding It back from expressing Its magnificence. We have leaders like Martin Luther King, Malala, and chained eagles to remind us.

General John Stark, the famous soldier of the American Revolutionary War, said it well: "Live free or die: Death is not the worst of evils."

When you lose your fear of death, you lose your fear of life. This. Right now. This one, tiny, log-and-chain or flying-eagle moment . . . It's yours. Only yours. Liberty or Death. You choose.

SHOW YOUR VALUE.

STEP THREE
CONNECTION
See Others' Value

CHARISMA RULE
See the great stuff others are made of.

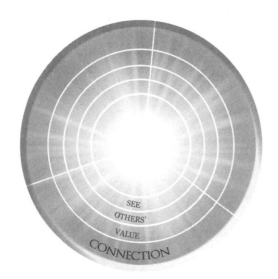

SEE
OTHERS'
VALUE
CONNECTION

"Everything has beauty, but not everyone sees it."

CONFUCIUS

I recently met with a member of the clergy at the Saint Sophia Cathedral in Los Angeles, in hopes of understanding the etymological roots of *charis* and "charisma" and how they are used in the Greek Orthodox tradition today. Father John gave me a thrill when he used his native tongue to give *charis* its proper audible expression.

"Khar'-ees," he said. I savored this virgin auditory experience.

I had been doting on, investigating, writing, and chopping up this little word for so long, all the while thinking it rhymed with Harris, only to discover it's more of a Clarice.

"Can you tell me about *charis* and charisma?" I asked.

With rays of afternoon light coming in through his little side chapel window, John eagerly engaged with my enthusiasm for his expertise.

"First of all," he said, "*charis* isn't used just in religious settings, but you are almost always giving it to someone. It can be a favor you do for them, like finding their keys, buying them some baklava, or wiping their tears. When people are filled with charisma during spiritual practice, they don't necessarily think they are giving it to others, but they are. They can't help it. They are like a fountain, and people want to be around them. After a meditation, I can always point to who was 'touched.' There might be a whole crowd of people, but the charismatic ones stand out to me. They glow. They don't have to do a thing; they simply attract others. But it doesn't last forever, you know. Sometimes you have charisma and sometimes you don't."

"In this tradition," I asked, "what practice do you do to get filled with charisma?"

In response, John handed me a little maroon and white booklet. "I think you will be interested in this," he said. "It is the prayer the mystic disciples of Jesus used in the desert. In prayer, it's not the words we say that matter; it's the space between them. We pray as a means to meditate and stop thinking about ourselves. The prayer helps us get out of our personal neurosis, and we experience *ékstasi* (ecstasy). That's when the gift of grace comes in and we get *khárisma*."

"What's that feel like?" I asked.

Smiling and with eyes aglow, he replied, "How can you explain what God feels like? I guess if I had to describe it, I would say it feels like love. But really big love. Really clear and really wide."

I prodded a little deeper. "If you had to use a word other than love, what would you use to describe your experience of being filled with *charis*?"

Without missing a beat, John replied:

"Connection."

It's time to spend your charisma currency! In this final chapter, we explore that ultimate frontier of the charismatic: personal interaction. This third step is chock-full of practical stories and exercises you can use to up-level your communication-and-connection finesse immediately. Combine this third step with the two previous and you will be able to connect with anyone, anywhere—regardless of cultural background or native tongue.

There's a reason this chapter is last. You've got to *know your value* (step one) and be willing to *show your value* (step two), before you can actually *give* anything of real value. When you enact steps one and two, people will perceive you as momentarily charismatic. In step three, you make your magnetism matter! It is in this third step that you will learn how to grow your influence and impact from fleeting to revolution-worthy. Steps one and two open doors. In step three, we walk through. Have you ever felt deeply misunderstood? This goes for companies too. Have you ever read your business's Yelp reviews and felt like your customers just don't get you? Even the most well-intentioned people and organizations poorly communicate who they are at times. The ability to effectively communicate yourself and your brand is a game changer. This chapter will show you how.

Although you've been interacting with humans all your life, there is still a good chance that, what with our present climate of social media and social expectations surrounding communication, you're not operating at your fullest flesh-and-blood, social-presence, charismatic potential. So, in the pages to come, let's relearn how to interact. We will do this by breaking down the stages of communication.

The recipe is simple: *Listen, Engage, Lead.*

When you listen as a charismatic, you become genuinely fascinated with your conversational partner. As described by Father John, true listening is an ecstatic practice, an escape from the confines of your own mind. Listening can set you free while simultaneously complimenting your conversational partner and releasing you from any obligation to entertain.

To up-level your listening skill, you will want to develop a habit of empathizing. Simply put on your partner's "boots." A charismatic's empathic feet can pull on anything: baby booties, Armani loafers, four-inch stacked stilettos, or the hard-won calluses of hoofing it barefoot. When you stand in their boots, you experience what your partner is experiencing. This can lead to gleaning the wisdom of 100 lifetimes in one. In addition to helping the listener to become a wise sage, listening is foundational to problem solving and leadership. I prescribe it as a cure for depression, anxiety, and pretty much every other modern psychosis.

After listening and establishing a foundation of empathy, you can *engage* in a sexy dialogue, which means a conversation that has no leader, just two people listening and responding to each other. You learn to play off of the person you are communicating with, like a musical duo, instead of trying to impress the person or force the conversation in a particular direction. As social creatures, we always feel more attracted to someone we are interacting with, as opposed to someone who is acting upon us. To optimize the full engagement potential in your conversations, listen for your conversational partner's level of engagement. Is your partner with you or not? As you develop your ability to track engagement or lack thereof, you become adept at altering your response in ways that keep your friend or customer with you! The only difference between deep communication and shallow communication is the level of engagement between parties. PS: Without engagement, revolution is futile.

After listening and engaging, and only then, can compelling leadership become possible. After some research into who your audience is and what their fears are, you will communicate from a platform of awareness and empathy, able to inspire them to be bigger, bolder, and more themselves. Here's a secret: when that happens, like it or not, people will want to follow your *lead*. Before we begin this next step—the step that bakes the charisma formula into a tasty tangible—I want to make sure we're with each other, that you're in my boots and I'm in your loafers. Please put a check next to the following items that are true for you:

You find yourself becoming

- ❑ A contagious person who's been granted special powers
- ❑ A sass-and-swag swinger who delights walking into rooms
- ❑ An Itster who's "Got the It"
- ❑ A fearless, high-flying, rebellious centenarian-to-be
- ❑ A bold innovator and diversity whore who enters stone soup cook-offs regularly
- ❑ A Madonna
- ❑ A head-shaking shaman and victory poser who's not afraid to touch others
- ❑ A meme-maker, better educated in culture than most yogurt makers
- ❑ One part copy-cat and one part god, alternating between mimicking and disrupting

❏ A mirror-staring lover who prays you'll become a
   narcissist one day or, at the very least, a pioneer fly

Check? Great. Congratulations. Now it's time to learn from
one of my favorite Charisma Code characters, the ox-tamer:

1. LISTEN

THE OX-TAMER

In a far-away northern county in the placid pastoral region,
Lives my farmer friend, the theme of my recitative, a famous
   tamer of oxen,
There they bring him the three-year-olds and the four-year-
   olds to break them,
He will take the wildest steer in the world and break him and
   tame him,
He will go fearless without any whip where the young
   bullock chafes up and down the yard,
The bullock's head tosses restless high in the air with raging
   eyes,
Yet see you! how soon his rage subsides—how soon this
   tamer tames him;
See you! on the farms hereabout a hundred oxen young and
   old, and he is the man who has tamed them,
They all know him, all are affectionate to him;
See you! some are such beautiful animals, so lofty looking;
Some are buff-color'd, some mottled, one has a white line
   running along his back, some are brindled,
Some have wide flaring horns (a good sign)—see you! the
   bright hides,
See, the two with stars on their foreheads—see, the round
   bodies and broad backs,
How straight and square they stand on their legs—what
   fine sagacious eyes!

How straight they watch their tamer—they wish him near
them—how they turn to look after him!
What yearning expression! how uneasy they are when he
moves away from them;
Now I marvel what it can be he appears to them, (books,
politics, poems, depart—all else departs,)
I confess I envy only his fascination—my silent, illiterate
friend,
Whom a hundred oxen love there in his life on farms,
In the northern county far, in the placid pastoral region.

WALT WHITMAN, LEAVES OF GRASS,
"DEATHBED" EDITION, 1892

What did the "famous tamer of oxen" use to do his taming? It wasn't whips or special calls, spurs, or barbed wire. Whitman's ox-tamer used the greatest disarming tool on earth. He *listened*.

The first ingredient of successful interaction is being able to listen. Truly, purely, without fear. Only when you can see your conversational partner through innocent eyes, can you actually *see* your partner and can your partner be seen. The ox-tamer was not looking for anything that wasn't there. He wasn't keeping an eye out for lack or malice, either. In other words, he did not project any expectations onto these wild beasts. He saw only what was there. As a result, the ox-tamer did not need to touch the oxen with words, whips, or an electric charge to get them to do his bidding. Humans respond in much the same way. Nothing gets us to relax, tell the truth, and get intimate better than when we feel like the person we are with sees us as we are. True charisma is as uncomplicated as this ox-tamer's "fascinated, silent, illiterate" mind. It sees the simple beauty in the beast. It's what gets you fed when you have no money in your pocket. It's the language you speak to let someone know you're with them. It makes people believe you're safe and trustworthy. It speaks from the corners of your eyes and the way you sit in your chair. We typically respond by trying to get closer to it, giving it a helping hand, or granting it access to well-guarded places. Indeed, the never-fail charisma key, the key that can be used in any country, with any species, the key requiring no words, can be summed up in two words: "See you." Olivia Fox Cabane observes that:

> The thing to remember is that some of the most charismatic people—such as Bill Clinton or Oprah Winfrey—are also the most disciplined, they pay an extreme amount of attention to what another person is saying and don't get distracted. That ability to listen intently and make a person feel like he or she is the most important one in the room is a key trait to learn if you want to be more charismatic.[1]

For many of us, being present is difficult enough by itself, let alone being present with another human being or a roomful of them. Yet, when someone is present with us, we feel fantastic. Being "seen" is all the oxen needed, or that any of us need, to feel at ease.

You can't fake interest, but you can genuinely choose to see. I cannot overestimate the importance of this concept. Your greatest social power will not come from bringing the best wine, wearing the nicest suit, or telling the best jokes. It will not come from a fabulous résumé or buying everyone dinner. Those are lovely gestures that may bring abundant joy to the lives of others, but what is most craved is simply to be heard, seen, and known.

When I am truly listening, I become porous. I am not pushing my rebuttals or judgments at the other person. I am not even *thinking* judgment and rebuttal. I am just listening, absorbing the other person and taking in what the person has to say as if he or she were a gourmet specialty I have yet to try. I become curious about what the person tastes like, how cooked or raw he or she is, how spicy or sweet. Don't mistake my description of a curious and porous demeanor as weak or wavering. When I'm getting my listen on, I'm intensely focused—so much so, there is a searing presence about me.

As I continue to listen in this way, the people I'm with brighten. They say things they've never said before. Under the influence of authentic listening power, they get a taste of their "something more." They get excited about the self-discovery and creativity flowing through them. I keep listening and asking questions to indicate that I want the "something more" they have, the "something more" they are. I'm genuinely interested. I do not always have this listening power, but when I do, people don't forget me.

Psychologists say that one of the most terrifying environments for folks to be in is at an interview or an audition where the interviewer or judge gives no emotive feedback. You tell a funny story, and they stare at you blankly, like a cold wall. You feel withered and shrunken. However, if the audience is really interested, you feel that too. You can tell they are with you.

A comic calls this a "warm room." We often give our best performances in warm-room environments. When we feel welcome, when we know we are wanted, we give more of ourselves, and we enjoy it.

I have met too many people who do not know how to listen. It is the saddest thing in the world to watch. They never get to experience being fully loved by anyone, because they don't even know whom they are with.

Your job as a charismatic listener is to help bring out the person (or people) you're with. Create the conditions in which they will feel wanted by not resisting them (not even in your thoughts!).

DEVELOPING INTUITION

Fifteen hundred years ago, the indigenous peoples of Oceania used the visceral power of listening to become master navigators. Without the aid of compasses or maps, they traveled thousands of miles in canoes with the same design and technology used in the Stone Age. With absolutely no charts or instruments, it would seem there was nothing to guide these ancient navigators to their destinations.

Although their primal navigation skills died quickly when these indigenous islanders were exposed to modern technology, one island within all of Oceania, Caroline Island, preserved the tradition. A few Westerners spent time with the keepers of these navigational mysteries, and they tell us that their ancestors taught themselves to navigate the seas by observing their environment, the way a diamond cutter observes the facets in the rocks.

Some 1500 years ago, these intrepid islanders lay on the bottom of their canoes, watching, feeling, listening, and tasting their way through the vast seas. They knew where they were by reading the currents, smelling the spray, and noticing the way the wind stirred their hair. They interpreted the flight of birds and how the phosphorescence in the water changed as they approached land. They watched the clouds for reflections of the shore, and touched the water to their lips to sense its temperature. To know where they were at all times, they followed the stars, reading the subtle messages of their world.[2]

The more we humans carefully observe our environment, the more we see what it's trying to tell us. When we teach ourselves to look for meaning in things beneath the surface, soon, we become master interpreters of our environment. As author Robert Greene says, "We know it from the inside and can sense the changes before they happen."[3] Like a dog who barks before an earthquake, the spider that feels the faintest strum of a gnat on the most outer edge of her web, or the revolutionary leader who knows the stirring of unrest in the crowd.

We've talked about listening and relating intimately to our environment, first as a tool for becoming present, and then for accessing greatness. I invite you to begin thinking about a further implication. The more acutely you listen like the Caroline Islanders, the more you can begin to read patterns. See around corners. Read the currents of your partner's energy. You begin to develop your intuition.

Intuition is simply listening turned up a notch, a vital tool for any leader, whether you lead a company, a family, a revolution, or your own life. As a growing charismatic, your intuition is one of the greatest assets you will develop. You'll be able to sense receptivity to connection, or the lack thereof. You will sense what others need.

The Oceania navigators' story touches me profoundly, because it speaks to the mastery available to us all when we choose to relate to people and things with sensitivity. However, we won't put in the effort it takes to develop this kind of sensitivity unless we feel that knowing the "other" is valuable. Only when we see that it's in our survival interest to know the other will we do what it takes to know them. This is human nature. These ancient navigators needed to know the sea as intimately as they did to stay alive.

We are quickly approaching a global civilization. It is in our own self-interest to *know the whole world*. We don't all see it—yet. When we know the places where we are actually intertwined, we seek to listen, see, and sensitively relate to and with a much broader spectrum of people and things.

Ready to have your mind blown? Our global civilization is not limited to the domain of world trade, internet connectivity, and the shared air we breathe. Data amassed by the Global Coherence Initiative clearly shows that humanity is affected by the earth's magnetic field on a global level. GCI also suggests that the earth's magnetic field acts as a carrier wave for emotional and other important biological information—thus connecting all of humanity and the earth. This group of bright researchers suggests that collectively our thoughts and especially our emotions create a "global information field" connecting us all.[4]

The Global Coherence Initiative data beg us to ask, "How connected are we, really?" When we choose to tune in and *listen*, we gain access to a cornucopia of information. Inspired by my time studying with these scientists, I began a daily practice: Before I go to bed each night, I ask myself, *What did I feed the field today? Was I present and caring? Did I listen? Did I wonder? Or was I judging, closed, scared, and fearful? What did I contribute?*

Most people today see the value of accessing virtual reality, because it's what we use to navigate around complex cities and get connected on social media. The virtual world gives us business transactions and introductions. It offers tools to make art. It provides filmmakers with their own production studio on a cell phone and free distribution channels on YouTube. It's what my team and I used to write this book. Lots of people even find their mates on virtual dating sites, but I will state the obvious: Only a very few get married without first finding out how they feel up-close and personal. We want to know that we're in love with someone. We want to viscerally feel whether we're a match or not—so we invest time. We listen. We become sensitive to our potential mate. Those couples who continue to value knowing their partner seem to enter a timeless love, the kind that feels like it could only deepen. Sagging and wrinkles are inconsequential to this kind of love. It is born from tangible experience, from putting in years of day-to-day, belly-to-belly, intuitive listening.

While you listen, remember to keep looking for the value in every moment. Dr. Rollin McCraty and his team at the Institute of HeartMath have shown that, beyond making us *feel* good, sustaining positive, heartfelt emotions opens us to receiving intuitive information. When I'm at ease in my heart, I'm available to listen for and receive the signs coming to me from my environment. If I'm keeping my eye out for the not so great, or if I'm distraught emotionally, I may want to push away the environment, instead of explore it. If I want to use my charismatic birthright to inspire engagement—if I want to connect with you—it will serve me to have information about your current emotional state. Dr. McCraty's research shows that I will be physiologically more receptive to how you are feeling if I can personally sustain positive heartfelt emotions.[5]

So, observe the environments you wish to master. When you activate your intuitive capacity through deep observation, listening, and sustaining positive heartfelt emotions, you unlock a life of fulfilling intimacy.

Try these exercises on for size:

1) **Separate sound tracks:** Experience your environment as if it had multiple "sound tracks" playing at once. There are birds chirping, leaves rustling, the water watering. Or maybe there's a car honking, people talking, and the dog barking. Wherever you are, see if you can separate the channels of sound around you as if you were identifying the different instruments in a song. This practice produces an ecstatic experience. Listening intently to your environment washes out your own cranium-confining thoughts. When you get the knack of this, you'll never want to stop. Give it a whirl right now!

Once you've got a hold on that one, try this:

2) **Listen to the sounds closest to you and then farther out:** One Buddhist meditation practice I like is called "big mind." Begin by listening to the sounds closest to you (your own breathing, family members in the other room) and then slowly widen your listening sphere until you are listening to the airplane overhead, then "hearing" the whole wide blue sky followed by the "sounds" of galaxies beyond.

3) **Seek out silence:** To balance your practice of listening in an environment bombarded with "instruments" playing over one another, take time out and seek quiet. Spend a few minutes every day marinating in the sanity

of silence. It will be as good for your physical health and creativity as it will be for your relationships. In the beginning was the Word; before the Word was . . .

As I've said, *listening* is not an ear-exclusive exercise. The kind of listening I'm urging you to develop is with your full sensory palate. Check this one out:

> 4) **Visual listening:** Look up from the page and take in the environment around you for five seconds. Now close your eyes. With your eyes still closed, recall what colors are to the right of you. What colors are to the left? What objects are in front of you?

You can also try this exercise next time you're with a friend. At a random moment, ask if he wants to play a game. Both of you will close your eyes, and while your eyes are still closed, take turns asking visual questions. For example, "What color are my eyes?" "How long is my hair?" "Am I wearing a watch?" "What kind of shoes am I wearing?" "What's my hottest feature?" (optional)

You now have exercises you can use any time to increase your auditory and visual "listening" skills. I invite you to explore *taste listening, touch listening,* and *scent listening* as well. There's one more sensory listening exercise I'd like to share with you. This one is my favorite. It is also the one that is most likely to get you laid, paid, and whatever else you want that rhymes. I call it "mood listening."

It goes like this:

> 5) The next time you watch a talk show or an interview program, pay close attention to the people talking. Try to label the exact moments when their moods change. *She was excited just a moment ago, wasn't she? Now she's crying. When did the shift happen?* Pay close attention to the changes in vocal tones and volume adjustments. Watch

for the slightest shifts in facial expressions. Practice this regularly, and you will develop a valuable connection skill. As if by magic, the world will begin to open its doors for you quicker than you can walk through. Why? Because you are literally *with* whoever you are mood listening to. Whatever doors are open to them become open to you; you are together.

EMPATHIZE

I have a story for you:

I was in my kitchen with my mom. I knew she'd been dealing with a health issue and was under a lot of stress. She was on edge today. I could hear it in her footsteps. When I tried to talk to her, I couldn't say anything right. When I lifted up my bare arm, she was staring at the flabby, soft under part with constricted pupils. I could feel her judgment. It was awful.

At one point during the visit, she said something mean to me. I don't even recall what it was, but at the time, it hurt. So I shot back, in anger, and suddenly, we were in the midst of a full-blown argument. The more we went on like this, the greater the negative sensations grew in my body. Problem was, the more I spewed the negativity with hopes I'd quell the sensations, the worse I felt.

Then I started praying, silently: *Please, help me. Help me to see this differently. I know she must be suffering to react this way today. Please help me see her as You do.*

My mom said the next defensive thing, and this time, instead of reacting with equal defense, I took a different tack. I blocked out her words, the ones that had been spinning me round in a game of right-or-wrong. In their place, I started listening to the feeling she was communicating.

Lo and behold, as I let myself feel her pain, my eyes and energy softened. I took the compassion I physically experienced and sent it as a kind of molten-gold energy, intending it to flood the space around and inside her.

When my mom finished her rant, I didn't say anything for a long time. I wanted it to register that I was now a safe harbor.

When I finally spoke, I said, "I hear you. I really do."

"You made me feel x, y, and z; terrible things!" she exclaimed.

"Oh, gosh," I replied, "I'm sorry. That wasn't my intention at all. I'm so sorry that you felt that way when I said that stuff."

I wasn't "putting on" the love. I had *chosen* to love and prayed that I could see through new eyes. I wanted to live the Great. Now I was able to genuinely give It to her. My mother paused. Her pupils dilated. Then, just like that, I had my full-hearted, loving mama back.

Later that day, my mom said goodbye to me. She looked me strongly in the eyes, and with great courage said, "I know I'm going to need to become the hero of my own story." My mother did become the hero of her own story. She courageously continued to stay open to possible solutions and found her health in the process.

Empathy is a miracle-making, conflict-resolving, relationship-forming, ecstatic practice. The word "ecstasy" originated from the Greek *ekstasis*, which literally means "standing outside oneself."

That's right, stand outside yourself ("ecstas-ize"), so you can stand in someone else's shoes (empathize).

In a very real sense, when you experience empathy for another, you get a free ticket out of yourself. You get to feel as if you were the other person. You do what your human nature is equipped to do. You ask, *"What if* I were Sara, and I was going through what she's going through?"

When you ask, the universe answers, filling your request. You start to feel Sara's experience as if it were your own. You put yourself in her moccasins and experience her perspective with all her history and circumstances. Like an actor, you step into the character of Sara and look at the world through that character's eyes.

Ahhh . . . sigh of relief . . . I don't have to be trapped in this brain and body. I can actually leave now and again and nothing terrible will happen. I'll get to give someone one of the greatest gifts we humans can give: the feeling of being felt.

"Feeling felt" is one of the primary tactics leading psychiatrist Mark Goulston uses with his clients. According to Goulston, the power of empathy has global consequences:

> In a now-legendary moment, President Ronald Reagan's talks with Soviet President Mikhail Gorbachev seemed to be at a standstill when Reagan looked behind his adversary's stubborn face to see a leader who truly loved his people. In a moment of brilliant simplicity, he invited Gorbachev to, "Call me Ron," (as opposed to, "Let's keep fighting president-to-president, digging our heels in and getting nowhere"). Gorbachev not only accepted the invitation, he joined Reagan in calling an end to the Cold War.[6]

How can simply making another "feel felt" lead to such huge changes of stance?

> **The Psychiatrist's answer:** "When people feel felt, they feel less alone, and when they feel less alone, they feel less anxious and afraid—and that opens them up to the message you're trying to send. They shift from defensiveness ("Get Away!") to reason, and they're capable of hearing your message and weighing it rationally."[7]

> **The Charismologist's answer:** "Feeling felt" is essentially the same thing as feeling connected. When we feel connected with another, we get a sense that we're on the same team. We drop our guard and become capable of collaboration.

WALK A MILE IN MY SHOES

Here's the skinny on how to walk a mile in another's shoes:

First, recognize that empathy is a vulnerable choice to make. As beloved teacher and therapist Dr. Brené Brown says, "In order to connect with you, I have to connect with something in myself that knows this feeling."[8]

I can think of so many times I've wanted to turn the other way to avoid feeling the heavy and dark emotions of those around me. I struggle most in this area with the people I'm closest to. It makes sense; these are the people I have trained myself to entrain with, and it takes work to not react negatively to their pain. There's a part of me that just wants to yell in righteous anger, "Don't bring me down with your bad mood!"

However, if we deny a person's pain, we miss out on seeing them. As a charismatic or as an ox-tamer, it is important to fill up on the various expressions of life by resisting as few as possible. Growing our stock of acceptable feelings in others makes us better able to disarm prickly defenses.

Every time I choose to feel what others are feeling—staying with them instead of trying to change, fix, or mitigate their pain—a softening occurs. So powerful is this softening on both the person in pain and myself that I know, without a doubt, that I am extending a transformational "gift of grace."

Dr. Brown suggests that when a person you are with is going through some dark clouds, reach out and gently tell them, "I don't even know what to say right now, but I'm just so glad you told me. Because the truth is, rarely can a fix-it response make something better. What makes something better is connection."[9]

We limit ourselves when we confine our problems to our personal ones. Once we get over ourselves, we can serve the big picture. When we start serving the big picture, we start playing the big game.

2. ENGAGE

Your conversation partner, the one you are ideally "unifying" with—be it a crush candidate, a potential employer, a customer, or an entire country—will respond best when you empower the person to be what we all are: a member of a superorganism society. Remember, we can't even source a cup of coffee alone. Have you any idea how many people it took to get that double latte into your hands? Farmers, pickers, truck drivers, airplane pilots, shop owners, cash register designers. The list is endless. While you may have felt you were "dying" for a cup, your literal survival depends on our ability to work together. In conversation, connect to our superorganism nature by inviting us to participate, collaborate, and create with you, and we will be far more receptive to what it is you have to say. You may find that, when you listen more, others listen more to you.

Acknowledging and "seeing" someone's pain does more than validate the person; it can also help you. Ever go through a rough time and a friend calls you asking for support? At first you may find yourself resistant, feeling you've got nothing to give and you don't want to fake a cheery face, but after helping her and hanging up the phone, you realize you're not so low anymore. How did this happen?

You became a vessel for kindness and encouragement. If you were a porcelain teapot, an empowering counsel brew flowed through your mouth spout and you got "stained" with it. You became what you relayed or related to. In addition, you engaged the ecstatic practice of empathy, standing outside yourself to feel your friend. When you hung up the phone and came back to yourself, you pushed the "reset" button on your bad mood. After you connected deeply with your friend, the neural pathways you "walked" shifted.

ADDRESSING FEAR (THEIRS AND YOURS)

First, let's address *their* fear:

"All great leaders," John Kenneth Galbraith tells us, "have had one characteristic in common: the willingness to confront unequivocally the major anxiety of their people in their time. This and not much else, is the essence of leadership."[10]

I dreamed of the Pope in a boxing ring. He was speaking from his Ultimate Fighting Championship ring to a full stadium. He said, "One way I always get on the books (meaning booked to speak) is I listen to what the fear is."

If you can listen for your audience's fear, you can address it. When you do, they will feel gotten, understood, and will pay attention, because they'll believe that what you have to say is relevant to them. Most important, you will be attempting to give your audience all any of us want, freedom from fear.

Discover your people's fears by asking them pointed questions. As an anthropologist, lifelong entrepreneur, and human whatifer, the question is my lifeline. I ask my people, whether friends, collaborators, or clients, what they fear. I ask directly and indirectly. Then I use my sensory listening skills to hear what it is they are *not* saying.

Now, let's address *your* fear:

The final important note on empathizing is to remember that nothing others do is about you. This may be the hardest idea to internalize, but it is true. We each go through life seeing through our own eyes and through the lenses of our experience.

Here's an extremely personal story to illustrate my point:

I'd ended a very passionate and soulful long-term relationship. A few months later, tender and yet full of hope and courage to meet the next chapter of my life, I began to date, but after every intimate encounter, I drove home sobbing. So sweet the tender heart, the body that brings the mind's cobwebbed corners to the surface of newly massaged flesh.

Then I met a man whom we will call Sam. I held Sam at bay for months before I let him in. When I did commit to physical surrender, it was short-lived and strange.

I wanted to punch him.

Part of me wishes I had. It would have opened the door to honesty instead of the incessant questioning in my head. Sam called once or twice but wouldn't see me again. During a long month of not seeing him, I spent countless hours wondering what was wrong with me. I'd let him in and he left. Why did *he* leave *me*? When we finally met face to face, he mentioned a quote by Don Miguel Ruiz that had been helpful to him: "Nothing others do is because of you. What others say and do is a projection of their own reality, their own dream."[11]

Helped him?

"That quote got me through you pulling away!" I exclaimed.

The universe is so tricky. Before I saw Sam again, the powers that be sent me another man, younger and more romantic; we'll call him Eric. After a beautiful evening of decadent food, tequila, roses, and adventure stories . . . he asked—no, begged—me to spend the night.

"Just rest up next to me," he offered. "In the morning you can go home and work."

"No," I said immediately. "I need to feed my cats."

He pulled me closer. "Please."

It did feel good to be near him. To be touched and held by a loving man who wanted me close. So I checked in with my body. My endorphins were on skin-high heaven from the cuddling and warmth. Still, my mind was freaking out. I was afraid to sleep over. I knew I would be forced to learn to relax next to him. The thought of grabbing my purse and leaving in a "you can't get me" flash felt freeing but also cowardly. So I asked myself: What's the biggest creative risk I can take right now? What's the most courageous choice I can make?

I stayed the night.

He was respectful, and I felt safe. Still, I couldn't sleep. While he slumbered beside me, I tossed and turned, a lion in a cage, muzzled and trapped. I lay there and prayed to be shown the way to nourishing sleep. How could I feel so trapped by this sweet sleeping man whose nice hair I'd been staring at for hours now?

Finally, near dawn and with nothing left to lose, I took my suffering self, isolated and cold in my own tension, and what did I do? I cuddled up to him and tried to connect. I put my heart right on him and breathed love into him. I even cooed a little. I was surprised to discover how much this relaxed me. Maybe, I thought, this tension is here because I don't fully believe we're on the same team. He could hurt me. Couldn't he?

All of a sudden, I had an insight into what had happened with Sam: *I bet he felt like I was feeling! Trapped and suffocated, unable to relax.* But he had chosen to pull away, and I now chose to stay. As young Eric lay there demonstrating every quality of a perfect sleeping companion, I had been unable to sleep. This time, it was me, not him! As I had shown up in all my glory with Sam, surrendered and trusting as best I was able, Sam hadn't shown up like I'd wanted him to. It was him, not me!

After the sun rose, I slept soundly for five hours in Eric's arms. When I awoke, I was highly energized. I was also proud of myself for sticking it through the ordeal of the dark night— for not leaving.

During the aforementioned face-to-face with Sam, though trembling and nervous, I told the story I just told you. I told him that, through my own recent encounters, I'd learned something about him.

Sam was moved by my boldness.

"This is real honesty," he said. "Thank you for telling me a truly honest story. Yes, I felt trapped. That is what happened." All awkwardness dissolved, and in the next beat, he called me family.

If someone does or says something that feels emotionally harmful, it cannot possibly be personal. The only thing that can ever be personal is love, because if you see someone clearly, you cannot help but love them! If you are not loving them, you are simply caught up in fear or numbness. If someone is not interacting with you in a compassionate way, they are not "seeing" you. Therefore, how could you take it personally? After all, you are made of great stuff!*

CREATING BRIDGES

To convey your message, you must first create a bridge on which you and your audience can walk together. You do this by establishing a line of communication. This takes practice and is a little like learning a language. With some folks it's easy; their language is similar to yours. With them, the conversation will flow. With others, you feel like you've landed in a foreign country without a guidebook. I'll use autism as an example of a language that may seem a bit surreal to you.

Autistic minds communicate with their world in a manner that, in contrast to the nonautistic mind, is heightened in many regards. The autistic mind has an extraordinary ability to pay attention, listen, and respond to the value in things that most nonautistic minds experience as lifeless. Often autistics will listen intently to the way water flows from a faucet or the way the wind touches their bodies, and then "speak" back with dance or song. In many cultures, a person with these exquisite skills has an exalted place in the tribe as a shaman, a medicine person, one who is known to communicate with parts of the world others cannot see. In other cultures they are drugged and institutionalized.

Busily trying to package, brand, number, and market our people and products in today's overly categorized, rationalized,

---

* Did you get that? Want to read it once more before moving on? I guarantee if you get this one concept in your bone marrow, nothing will ever be the same.

and industrialized society leads us to labeling autistic people as "handicapped." Even with a culture nipping at the bit to move faster-faster-faster in precise "know-it-all" boxes, I see only one real barrier to integrating the autistic and the nonautistic into a functioning superorganism society: Nonautistic minds and autistic minds have not yet learned to speak each other's languages.

Charisma is nothing—no "gift of grace," no "soul's jewelry" or "currency of connection"—if it does not first establish a working line of communication. It is imperative that you respond to your conversation partner in a way that shows you have been listening to him or her. Watch for your partner's ideal style of communication, and activate your mirror neurons!* Mirror neurons activate when people observe each other. They are linked closely with the experience of empathy, causing the same areas that are activated in one person's brain to become activated in the partner's brain. Mirror neurons are thought to be the primary biological feature allowing us to empathize with others. When you "take a walk in someone else's shoes," you literally undergo measurable changes in your brain. It's a natural phenomenon. The brain cannot tell the difference between actually doing something and seeing it done. For example, if you see someone's arm break, you cringe, on some level imagining the same thing happening to you.

How do mirror neurons help you communicate? Two ways: First, when you mimic someone's body language, emotions, speech patterns, and facial expressions, you get the inside scoop on who that person is—beyond what they're telling you. As

---

* In the autistic mind, the mirror neuron system is considered to be "dysfunctional." This does not preclude that these individuals are not craving to be connected with. Nor does it preclude that they do not have different, just as intimate ways of connecting with and reading their environment. The same is true for psychopaths who are believed to be born with mirror neurons that act as one-way instead of two-way mirrors. This means that the psychopath sees you well enough to mimic and manipulate you but does not experience you as a vicarious mirror when they are looking in your eyes. In other words, the psychopath is biologically born not to feel for the person he or she is seeing.

you mimic, your mirror neurons literally allow you to feel what they're feeling. Useful info to have when looking to connect with someone, no? Second, the people you mirror are more likely to trust you, sensing that you understand them, are like them, and are part of their tribe. Truth is, you may or may not be part of their tribe. But you are listening! Planning on leading a team anytime soon? Inspire the power of collaboration by mirroring and mimicking your people.

Check out this revealing, recent research on the social power of mimicking: In the experiment, volunteers were asked for their opinions on a series of advertisements. A member from the research team subtly mimicked half the participants. A few minutes later the researcher "accidently" dropped six pens on the floor. The participants who had been mimicked were found to be two to three times more likely to pick up the dropped pens. The study concluded that mimicry had not only increased good will towards the researcher in a matter of minutes but had also prompted an increased social awareness and group connectivity.[12]

PLAYING JAZZ

The best way to lead is to interact. Trust is formed when people feel they are having a conversation with you. Not at you, not for you, but collaboratively. In the grooviest of groovy relationships, there's very little distinction between the caller and the responder. You may be the highest integrity person on the planet, but if you don't elicit trust, those around you will never let you into the intimate territory of their hearts, minds, and lives. So when you do speak, wait for it; don't jump the gun. Learn from collaborative Greats like Dizzy Gillespie, John Coltrane, and Ella Fitzgerald. Learn to play jazz.

As any jazz musician knows, you find the groove by listening and responding to your jam mates. Inspiration is born from taking in another musician and letting that musician spark your next note. Verbal conversation is similar. Good conversation comes from deep listening, which facilitates your ability to respond in relationship to whomever you are speaking with.

Often we think we have to engage in what I call the "Jack-off Olympics" to get the respect we're searching for. "This is me! Listen to me! These are all the things I've done, and this is where I'm going!"

Don't do this.

If you are trying to impress someone, I guarantee they will be more impressed by your interest than by some fancy story. Communication becomes a regenerative art only when you become more interested in discovery than in regurgitated identity. No scripts or premeditated choreographies are required for jazzy conversations. It's a moment-to-moment, spontaneous unfolding of ideas.

The reality of our societal "orchestra" is profound. Is humanity's music always harmonious? No. But we still pick up our violins and our trombones, our laptops and our eighteen-wheelers and work together the best we know how.

Through conversation, subtly remind us of how you need us. Remind us of the ways we add value to your life. Remind us of the part we play, and we will want to make music with you. We humans like to feel important, you know!

Of course, you can't remind us of the music we play unless you listen to it. Not only that, if you don't listen to my "music," you'll never be able to figure out how to interlock parts with me. And in that case, you can say goodbye to getting laid or paid. When in doubt, ask a question.

MONOLOGUE VS. DIALOGUE

I recently received a coaching call offered as a complimentary appetizer to entice a full-program purchase. Half an hour into the call, I was ready to buy. This coach was *with* me, asking me perfect questions that had me crying epiphanies. However, at the end of the call, when he started pitching his program, he stopped playing jazz and started playing Jack-off Olympics. I remember feeling shocked on the other end of the phone, tears of awesome vulnerability still fresh on my face. Doing what he had to do to make his sale, the coach had *left me* cold. This was his moment to sell to me, tell me everything, and win my credit card! The thing is, I was ready to buy before his one-sided pitch, because of our connection. I hardly cared what the deal was. When this coach began rambling on with a ten-minute monologue pitch, never asking a question to see if I was still with him, he lost the sale.

Features, benefits, fancy deals, and shining testimonials are garbage if they override connection and dialogue. Feel nervous? Don't keep talking. Stop. Take a breath and ask a question to find out what's going on with the person you feel nervous with.

Dr. Martin Luther King regularly spoke about the threat of monologue on society. He knew that if we do not engage in dialogue with the people who see things differently than we do, we put ourselves in danger of creating mental stances and prejudices based on ignorance over truth. Anytime conversation becomes one directional (a monologue) it loses touch with reality. If you want to know what's really going on when you find yourself in conflict with a lover or in a war zone, engage in dialogue with everyone. Just as you are not the thoughts you think about yourself, others are probably not what you think about them. Replace assumptions and declarations with questions. Play jazz.

If you want peace, you don't talk to your friends.
You talk to your enemies.
MOSHE DAYAN, ISRAELI GENERAL AND POLITICIAN
(1915–1981)

Here is a good example of two people who could not play jazz together:

His name was Derek. He was one of my more eccentric college boyfriends, a six-foot-four-inch music student who knitted his own shoes. He made stained-glass pieces for me and lived on the UCSC campus in the hollow of a lightning-struck redwood tree. This boy-man was deep.

My mother still tells the story of when I brought Derek home to meet her: "He didn't even shake my hand or introduce himself. He just nodded, walked past me into my living room, and started turning circles, dancing. What was he dancing to, Robin?" From that day forward, whenever I brought a boyfriend home, she would say with a laugh, "Well, at least that one didn't dance in my living room!"

After that initial meeting, Derek's many gifts were wasted on my mother. He sent her a package of crayons and papers with a colorful, scribbly card that Hallmark would have fainted over. I thought it was a lovely gesture; my mother said it looked like a wrapped bomb.

I can only imagine Derek in grade school; I think he would have knocked everything over—on purpose. That was his charm. The only thing missing was that he didn't find value in others receiving his eccentricity.

It is true that *not everyone is going to like you*. However, if you want to gift your gifts, you will need to create the circumstances for your gifts to be received. You must elicit trust and receptivity. How is that done? By learning the language of others.

What if Derek had taken the time to learn my mother's language before he turned our living room into a dance hall? What dance might have transpired then? What if my mom had chosen to learn his language and joined in his celebration?

There is no right way. There is nothing one-directional about life. We live in a world of call and response, so burn the script and get into the charisma groove by being brave enough to allow whatever spontaneous thing is happening in your environment to happen to you.

It takes guts to wait for my dance partner to move me;
I have to let go of control;
He could drop me, step on my foot, miss the turn,
or leave me to spin alone
But it's only when I let my partner show up
That the real dance begins.
If I don't, we will both end up
at the Jack-off Olympics
Trying, in desperation, to get in.
Groove needs something to groove to.

Practice tying these concepts together:

1) Listen for the language your receiver speaks. This is fun! Seek to know what you don't yet understand in whomever you are seeking to communicate with. In this practice, you get to enter another's world. If, for example, an autistic person is waving his or her hands around in ways that make absolutely no sense to you, try waving your own hands around and discover a whole new world of making jazz with the wind. Mimic the autistic person's still-strange-to-you responses. Pay attention to your goal in doing this: You are seeking to learn a new language. You are seeking to learn *the person's* language.

2) "Speak" the new language you're learning. As I've said over and over again and will forever continue to say, all living things respond to being seen for what they are. If you're a good mimic, the person you're mimicking will more than likely assume you're like him or her, with all the culture and life experience that goes along with that. As mentioned earlier, the person will instinctively feel you are part of his or her tribe and will respond with instinctual trust.

When I was in preschool, the nearby school of young children with Down syndrome visited us every Friday. The teachers' idea of mixing the "normal" kids with the "special" kids was an attempt to foster compassion and appreciation of differences. My family uses the class photos from that year as laughter-inducing antidepressants. The first photo shows the "normal" kids interspersed with the "special" kids. In it, my tongue appears to be too big for my mouth, and I'm slouched over, sandwiched between two Down syndrome kids who looked just like me. I don't recall why I mirrored my "special" friends that day. My image seems to say, "I'm like you; I'm one of you." The second picture, taken a moment later, included only my primary class of so-called "normal" children. In that one I'm sitting tall and smiling bright. I look like all the other kids in that photo too. Still saying, *I'm like you. I'm one of you.*

3) Enjoy the fearlessness that comes with giving the gift of attention. When your attention moves from you to someone else, your self-consciousness goes away. Revel in empathy's out-of-body high, trying on different personas and perspectives. You will not lose yourself. You will grow your impact through engagement.

"Introspection is out and outro-spection is in."[13] So says philosopher and author Roman Krznaric, as he explains how we can help drive social change by stepping outside ourselves. Krznaric suggests we train ourselves to get into strange shoes by becoming an empathic adventurer.

Begin by cultivating your curiosity about strangers. Ask questions, try on their way, observe, see, and play with them in their world. *Oy vey*! You will be so loved. At the very least, you will stretch the boundaries of your little self and get a little closer to your Self. I wholeheartedly agree with Krznaric's insights: by trying on the lives of others, you grow your ability to think creatively, you improve your relationships, and you create the human bonds that make life worth living.[14]

4) Be an empathic revolutionary. Empathy is not only for one-on-one situations. It can be a collective force and has powered many revolutionary social movements. If we don't hang out in the majesty of rain forests, it's hard to prioritize protecting them. Even if we intellectually know that chopping down the Amazon at a rate of an acre per second is killing us and the planet, the real motivation to protect walks hand in hand with experiential, bark-to-belly connection. *We protect what we feel connected to.*

Please listen keenly to the words of Mr. Krznaric here. These are words I take to heart as I work with top executives, venture capitalists, and corporations:

> We normally think about empathy as empathizing with the down and out, the poor and marginalized, those on the edges of society. I think we need to be more adventurous in who we try to empathize with. I think we need to empathize with those in power. We need to understand how those in power think about the world, their lives and their ambitions. We need to understand their values. Only then are we going to be able to develop effective strategies for social, political and economic transformation.[15]

Which brings us to our next section . . .

3. LEAD

A Leadership Vision is a cluster of metaphors, concepts and stories that uncannily point to a future that feels at once strange and familiar and that is clearly better than the present. So articulated, the vision inspires action, creation, and engagement.

DR. MARJORIE HASS, PRESIDENT OF AUSTIN COLLEGE

The precursors to leadership are listening and engagement. Walt Whitman's "Ox-Tamer" and my "Pope in a boxing ring" have taught you the rules for listening and engaging. You are now prepped to lead. One of the biggest misperceptions about leadership is that all it requires is character, position, and vision. Of course, these qualities are part of the leadership cocktail, but without listening and engaging, you will be left with an empty cocktail glass.

Dwight D. Eisenhower defined leadership as "the art of getting someone else to do something you want done because he wants to do it."[16] This brings us to a delicate subject—the distinction between leadership and manipulation.

I recently heard the following definition of "evil": evil is making someone do what they don't want to do. What's the difference between that and manipulation? I'm not entirely sure, but you'll want to consider it when residing in a position of power (whether you're a mother or a father, a boss, a celebrity, or a government agency). The difference between leadership and manipulation is the difference between inspiring someone and forcing them. The art of charismatic leadership is knowing whom you're leading so you can paint a vision that excites you both. The manipulator does not care who does it, only that you do what the manipulator wants.

In the Tao Te Ching, Lao Tzu says, "A leader is best when people barely know he exists; when his work is done, his aim fulfilled, they will say: 'We did it ourselves.'" How? By shifting your perspective from leader-as-knower to leader-as-learner. To step into the role of leader-as-learner you must ask *questions*. Many questions. Begin by asking yourself, "What can I learn from my people that will allow me to lead them more effectively?" Become interested in the lives of your people. Ask them what they value about the topic at hand. Ask them what challenges they are facing. Ask them what ideas they have to make it better. Instead of making your people wrong for perceived failures, ask them questions about what *went* wrong. Give up punishment and gain connection. Your job is to become more interested in discovering and fixing the broken link than to keep a ledger for bad stuff.

> *If I am walking with two other men, each of them will serve as my teacher. I will pick out the good points of the one and imitate them, and the bad points of the other and correct them in myself.*
> CONFUCIUS

The corporate powerhouse of innovation, Google, uses team failures as models for future growth. If we are to walk in the footsteps of the great sage Confucius, we will openly broadcast both the successes and failures of individuals within our team, so that our entire superorganism can intelligently choose to either mimic or correct its actions accordingly.

Inspire your people to "want to do what you want them to do" by sharing power *with* them instead of holding power *over* them. Power over is too much gosh-darn responsibility for a leader. Your shoulders will feel like lead and your problems will only grow. You can't muscle a superorganism into effectiveness, but you can give everyone a part they are proud to play.

Let me paint this more clearly with a story:

A while back, I emceed a weekend event for a big-name speaker and coach. My job was to warm up the room before the speaker entered. I began each morning and ended each break by getting the 200 attendees to dance. During the first half of the first day, the group gladly followed my lead, because it dispelled their awkwardness in a room of people they didn't know. By the second half of the first day, their comfort and familiarity with one another had increased so much, they no longer did a thing I requested. They chatted instead of following my less-than-seductive invitation to move their bodies with me. I began to wonder if my mic had broken. Finding little pleasure in screaming at a room to follow the wiggle of my hips, I started the next morning with something a little different. I decided to educate them about the superorganism. I told them how unique humans are as a superorganism species and how we can access that superpower together by synchronizing and aligning our movements and purpose. I asked if they wanted to join me in an experiment to see how strong a group mind we could create by matching our own movements to the dancing body onstage. They cheered emphatically. Then I told them I would be picking random people to come onstage and lead us in movement. The room had been quiet before; now it went silent. I'd raised the stakes. I intentionally took them out of their comfort zone. I also gave them a reason to play along: They were part of an experiment. They wanted to explore this group engagement technology that I had just finished telling them was as old as their earliest ancestor and as recognizable as the military march. As you learned in "Step One: Confidence," it is often the process of overcoming fear and struggle that leads to perceiving an experience as valuable. If we overcome that fear as a group, the group becomes strong as well. In addition, adding elements of surprise, risk, and discovery keeps engagement high. By the end of the exercise, I could barely keep them off the platform.

As my dear friend and master magician Jeff McBride says, "If you want people to participate, give everyone a part," but here's the question every great leader must have asked at one point during their journey towards leadership: "How can I possibly assign parts if I don't first listen to what people play best?" In the story I just told you, I watched my group closely to identify who would best serve the group before I called anyone to take the stage. What are we doing in this step of *The Charisma Code*? That's right: learning to *see others' value.*

CHECK YOUR EXPECTATIONS

How well do your people play their parts? Ever wanted to increase your team's performance? Hold onto your seatbelt, because the findings of the following experiment, used consciously, will have a Midas effect on your team, increasing the value of everyone you touch!

Once upon a time, researchers gave teachers a list of students indicating which incoming students were high achievers. The teachers were told to expect outstanding performances by the specified students. Sure enough, by the end of the year, these students' IQ scores increased dramatically. But it turns out the researchers had actually chosen these students at random! What happened? The "Pygmalion effect" happened, that's what! The Pygmalion effect is a phrase used to describe the phenomenon that occurs when higher expectations lead to an increase in performance. The teachers believed in the students marked as high achievers. In response, those students grew into high achievers. Whoa... The students were never told in words that they were high achievers. But somehow, using a language beyond words, the teachers powerfully communicated their belief in the chosen students.[17] Was it the teacher's warm and encouraging body language? Yes. Did they give more positive attention, feedback, and learning opportunities to these students? Yes. Maybe more smiles, nods, and eye contact? I'm sure of it. Was it a subtle energetic belief that made a space for grace? I believe so, yes.

How can you use the Pygmalion effect with the people you lead? Regularly return to this one-liner from James Rhem, executive editor for the online National Teaching and Learning Forum: "How we believe the world is and what we honestly think it can become have powerful effects on how things will turn out."

Beware: the opposite of the Pygmalion effect, called the golem effect, wherein low expectations lead to low performance, also occurs. Check your expectations.

Wanna play? Of course you do. The Pygmalion effect is not just for kids in a classroom. Tel Aviv University professor Dov Eden has shown the power of the Pygmalion effect through all industries and work groups. Dov Eden says, "It sounds so simple; it seems too good to be true." And yet, a recent statistical analysis combining the results of many studies found that Pygmalion leadership training was the most effective leadership development intervention.[18] Go on now, raise the bar on what your people can do, solve, and create!

Next time you are collaborating with a group, practice looking for each individual's value. Wait, don't just practice, prioritize it! This search will help you genuinely hold high expectations for your people. The kind of genuine expectations that will communicate, through a language beyond words, that you *see the great stuff others are made of.*

The result: hidden gold, not so hidden anymore.

THE GOLDEN RULE

The teachings in this book are a product of the Golden Rule.

The Golden Rule is very simple: "Do unto others as you would have them do unto you."[19] Although that's a direct quote from the Bible, it's interesting to note that every religious tradition has, at its heart, a version of the Golden Rule. Although it may sound simplistic and possibly even Pollyanna-ish, I highly encourage you to incorporate it into the core of your leadership style. "Treat others as you would like to be treated" assumes that you *know your self.* In a tough situation, whether with an employee or a CEO, you might ask, "How would *I* like to be treated in this situation?" When you answer honestly, you may find that a direct confrontation is what you would want. The motivating factor that inspires us to "treat others the way we would like to be treated" isn't that the Bible, the Qur'an, or the Torah told us to do so. It comes from genuinely seeing people's value. When we *see others' value,* we *want* to treat them well.

But there's more. *The Charisma Code* expands the Golden Rule: Do unto others as you would have them do unto you; what you do to others, you do to yourself. It's the coffeepot concept. Recall how the porcelain coffeepot gets heated and stained when hot, black coffee is poured through its spout. We. Are. Connected. Best you lead and live like it.

Want to take this interconnectivity concept from the lofty and practice it in the real? Here's the deal. Besides noticing how you feel with every action you pour from your "spout," next time you see someone on the side of the road whose eyes and posture, dress and sign indicate the person is hungry, say to yourself, "Look, I'm hungry." When you see someone in pain, say, "Look, I'm in pain." When you see someone jumping for joy in total celebration, say to yourself, "Look, I'm celebrating!"

Whether your title says you are a leader or a follower, you are always setting an example of something. As we've discussed, in any given moment, you are either adding to, subtracting from, or making new memes. Let's consider two extremely influential cultural group practices. One of these behaviors is the most destructive for organizations, and the other is one of the most constructive.

MOST DESTRUCTIVE: GOSSIP

When you set an example that gossip is an acceptable form of behavior, watch out! That s——t can eat the entire fabric of a once-thriving organization. Yet we feel compelled to gossip. It's like the first drink of the night; you get a buzz from the stuff at first, but if you keep spouting out the bad will, you and everyone involved will become very ill. This is an example of the Golden Rule at work. Treat others poorly by speaking poorly about them behind their back and it will turn around and hurt the workings of you and your system.

Gossip is unhealthy for any group, be it a classroom, couple, or company; but, as you know from step one, we have the power to repattern any pattern! One way to turn your gossip into productive talk is to grow the balls needed to confront people directly. Courageous communication brings health, trust, and transparency to the table. But don't stop with the stuff that's hard to address; become a sugar queen or king and edify everyone around you! If you're a leader, this will get you followed; if you're an employee, this will get you promoted. Ultimately, though, it doesn't matter who you are; if you spout out good will, you'll feel really good!

MOST CONSTRUCTIVE: CRITICAL THINKING

When you set an example that others are valuable to you by asking them questions and encouraging them to ask questions, good news! This is an excellent use of the Pygmalion effect. You demonstrate confidence in your people when you ask them questions that matter. This will lead to a culture that nourishes critical thinking, as opposed to a content-dumping culture, which leads to complacency and dullness. Do all you can to set an example of critical thinking, and expect to see the levels of your people's engagement, enthusiasm, and effectiveness rise through the skylight!

GO THERE FIRST!

You may ask, "What about *my vision*? I mean, I've got a responsibility to direct my ship towards a common goal. With all this listening and assigning of parts and invitation for questioning and group participation, as well as campaigning for risk and discovery while burning my 'bad stuff' ledger, I'm beginning to imagine my ship without a rudder." I hear you.

What I'm about to tell you will not add any more safety to your sailing outfit, but it will get your people excited to join you on your mission. Expect more buy-ins and more courageous followers. Direction alone will not get you to your destination. Nor will it enlist a team. If you want someone to go somewhere, you must go there first! As the Chinese proverb points out, "Not the cry, but the flight of a wild duck, leads the flock to fly and follow," and in the words of Ken Keyes, author of *The Hundredth Monkey* as well as numerous other books, "You don't lead by pointing and telling people someplace to go. You lead by going to that place and making a case."[20]

Bees, one of our fellow superorganisms, demonstrate this leadership strategy in the "honeybee waggle dance." In it, worker bees go out scouting in different directions for a food source or a new home. When they return, they take turns dancing for the rest of the hive. Using infinity figure (∞) patterns and waggles that mark in degrees what angle from the sun their find is, the bees communicate the location. This dance tells not only the direction to go in, but how good they think the spot is. The strongest dancers convince the other bees that their newly found food source or home site is worthy of exploration. As other bees go out to investigate the worthiness of the new find, they come back to the hive and perform the dance too. When enough bees are doing the same dance, a threshold is crossed. The whole hive picks up and goes!

Moral of the story: If you want your people to go somewhere, go there first and get good at communicating how great it is!

This leads us to our next topic: How to speak charisma code to captivate attention, inspire action, and solicit buy-in. Or, how to do a human waggle dance.

Are you ready?

SPEAK

First, you must pick an audience and speak to them
in language that fits their understanding of the world.
Second, you must speak to them from the heart.
If you follow both criteria, you will not be wrong.
EMAIL FROM MY FATHER

Before we go any further, stop and ask yourself: "What do I have to offer others that I know will be of value to them, that I know will bring some relief, some answer to a gnawing problem, to a joyless heart, to a confused soul, to a hopeless life, to desperation? What gift of grace am I primed to give?"

As I once heard über-successful, transformational writer and speaker Lisa Nichols say, "Speak to serve instead of speak to sell." Indeed. The Golden Rule loves to boomerang money and clients to those who genuinely seek to serve.

Before you can confidently serve it up, you first have to know you have something of value to give. No amount of reading this book will get you to believe. You must do the confrontational work of asking yourself how you can serve the world. When you seek to answer this question, does your heart race? Do your palms get sweaty? Do you blank out? Do you think it's for "other people"? Keep asking. When you believe you have something valuable to share, people change the way they respond to you. They begin sitting on the edge of their seats to hear what it is you have to say.

When you know you have the ability and desire to provide value to others' lives, it becomes the motivation behind your every word. At this point two things happen:

- Your anxiety drops. You realize you are not there to be judged. You're not seeking approval; you're offering service.
- You have fun!

Standing in front of a stadium of thousands or asking that gal to grab some scrumptious eats becomes natural when you believe you've got great stuff to give; the kind of stuff that's going to improve someone else's life. When you truly know this, inhibitions drop away. You're no longer trying to sell something or get something. Your purpose becomes laser focused on providing value!

Just like our honeybee wagglers, the strongest dance wins! The best dancing bees communicate that they have something valuable to share because—and only because—they actually do have something valuable to share! The honeybee's conviction is enough to get their tails wagging dynamically, and that dynamic waggle is what eventually leads to an entire hive's movement. So, when you are ready, speak dynamically. When you speak dynamically, you let "the jewelry of your human soul" out of its closet (your body) and into the territory of the living (everything outside your body). In other words, you communicate from the inside out. You communicate with Soul Force. Charisma's magnetism is bred from that ability to make the inner part of yourself visible to others in such a way that it compels and engages them.

Soul is not tightly collared; it needs an expansive playground to cavort in. One tone simply will not do. Soul rises from within. As it reaches the surface of your bodily orifices, it widens your eyes, takes in breath, and lets out words in strings of melody. Soul has a tendency to draw your shoulders back and stick your chest out. But it's not bravado. It's just so ready to give of itself, because Soul knows its value.

Let's explore some methods of creating dynamic, soulful communication.

THE CHARISMATIC SPEAKER

Your job as a charismatic speaker, should you *choose* to be one, is to shake people up. You first create trust, attention, and rapport by using the listening and engagement skills you've been learning in this chapter. Next, you swoop into your audience's hearts and minds, giving them an experience of what's possible! Most people live a dull, small sector of their life's potential. Deadened and boxed into a monotone mundane, they think tiny thoughts and feel tiny feelings. Dynamic, soulful communication is a way to break through their limited confines while providing a glimpse of an extraordinary alternative.

The charismatic speaker is no Lilliputian.

How do you become a charismatic speaker?

In review, here's an easy-peasy quick guide:

- Create rapport with your audience by using your listening and engagement skills.
- Identify what you can give your audience that will add value to their lives.
- Shake your people up with an experience of what life can be like!

Don't know what your people want? Here's another cheat sheet for you. Everyone wants the following things:

- The Removal of Fear and Anxiety
- Connection
- Belonging
- The Feeling of Aliveness
- Feeling Valued, Recognized, Needed and Seen as Special
- Personal Power and Independence
- Being Part of Something Larger than Themselves
- The Removal of Limitation
- Feeling Cared For
- Strategies for Getting Laid or Paid
- Feeling Loved
- Feeling Free

Don't you want these things? Teapot, people. Remember the teapot. Tip it and pour the above list through your "spout," and see what happens. *You become what you relate to.*

TELL A STORY

Those who tell the stories rule society.

PLATO

A good story invites us into another world. It gives us someone else's perspective and is one of the most important connection tools for anyone seeking to use their words to influence, make an impact, and change the world. With that highfalutin statement behind me, I will move on and say that stories are absolutely *not* necessary for changing the world. Rocking an engaging language beyond words will get you much further on its own. With that said, if you happen to be speaking with people who are fluent in the language you speak, stories, told properly and kept short, can be a tool through which to channel your charisma. WARNING: Stories, by their very nature, draw from the past. Danger! Danger! The antithesis of charisma is disassociating with the here and now. *Itster*, remember? Avoid this whammy of a potential storytelling pit by regularly connecting what happened then to what's happening now. Fear telling a past-participle monologue— exchange it for the pulsing presence of Here and Now by regularly relating your story to yours and your audience's current shared experience. If the story was about the Great Depression, how does that relate to today's market? Don't wait till the end of a saga to make the connection. Whenever possible, tell us as you go along. This is likely to keep us more engaged. When you're communicating, your conversational partner's engagement level should be one of your top priorities.

Still, we humans love stories. They stick longer than bare facts. So if you feel moved to say something, consider checking your back pocket for a story you can pull out to help communicate your thoughts. Caveat to add to my prior warning: there is such a thing as a bad story. You know the ones. They go something like this: "Have you seen that movie? Oh gosh, what was it called, oh shoot, I can't remember right now. Wait, that's right, it's called *When Michelangelo Dated the Princess with the Yellow Toenails!*"

"No," you respond. "Must have missed that one."

"Well," your conversation partner continues, "What you just said reminded me of something in that movie. You see there was this guy and there was this girl. The guy tried really hard to get the girl, so he painted some big ceiling but then fell in love with God, and there was something about the girl's toenails that reminded me of the struggle you just told me about in reference to your mother's dying last month. (*Awkward pause*) I guess you'd need to see the movie to understand what I'm talking about. . ." *Moral of the Bad Story:* Never try to recreate the storyline of a piece of media for someone who's never seen or read what you are referring to. If they've previously consumed the media you're talking about, great! Move forward with your story using the media as a reference for your point. If they have not seen the film or read the book, let it go. Do not try to recreate a story that took the creators years of thought and millions of dollars to make engaging and communicable.

TIPS FOR TELLING A GREAT STORY

Telling a great story is pretty simple. Keep it short, keep it personal, and use it as a tool to give heart, credibility, and possibly humor to the factual information you wish to convey. Bullet points:

- Use colorful metaphors, similes, poetry, visionary imagery, and lots of heart.

- Remember: all language is metaphor, because words are simply labels for things that exist in the world. We call something "a book" because we have to call it something, but the word is not the thing it names.

- Draw your audience into the present with sensory details. Don't tell us; show us. We want to eat the food, not the menu: *The girl in polka dots huddled in the corner of the classroom, head buried in her tiny arms, while a group of adults towered over her in heavy woolen brown and black coats.*

- Share the character's obstacles and barriers, so your listeners' inner heroes get a chance to experience what the character must overcome. As I once heard in a story-telling workshop, "Superman without kryptonite is boring."

- Use explicit metaphors as a means to bypass cognition by bringing two unlike things together, showing that they have something in common. This kind of communication results in feeling, not concept. For example, "Between the lower-east-side tenements, the sky is a snotty handkerchief."

- Place connection first! How close can you get to your listener? As you speak, seek to bring them into the story, as if the two of you are reliving it together. Instead of: "My husband told me to pick up my bags and leave forever," you might say something like: "My husband looked at me with eyes so cold and pointed, I thought I might turn to stone. I couldn't move. Yelling frenetically, he flung open my dresser drawer and began throwing handfuls of my lingerie, demanding I leave immediately."

Q: What is "the gift of grace" someone brings when they speak this way?

A: They remind us that we are not alone. They remind us of our shared human experience.

THE TAKEAWAY

The most engaging forms of communication are those where your listener gets to live what you're describing and feel what you're feeling. Paint a picture for them. Let your emotions color the canvas. When you touch a person's heart, you have the person's attention. When you have someone's attention, you can use it for transformation. That's power. An engaging, personal life story takes your experience and gives it to someone in its raw, untamed truth. Whoever is so lucky to receive your most daring stories gets the balm of intimacy rubbed into their sore, isolated souls. With a good tale, you spend connection currency and become seriously rich in return. *Take off your shoes and let your listeners walk in them.*

FORMULA FOR STRUCTURING STORIES THAT YOUR LISTENERS CAN TAKE ACTION ON:

1) *Reason:* Begin by giving your listeners a reason why you are going to tell your story. That is, how will it help them?

2) *Story:* Tell your story in its entire emotional, belly-to-belly, soul-to-soul, visceral, visual, transformational, see-through glory.

3) *Moral:* Share what you learned from the experience you're recounting, so your listeners will have a takeaway touchstone for applying its wisdom.

TWO IMPORTANT ACCESSORIES TO BRING WITH YOU ON THE STORYTELLING STAGE:

● *Eye Contact:* Eyeballs are connection portals. Practice speaking the language beyond words by imagining you are spinning threads, like a spider, between your eyes and the person whose eyes you are communicating with.

● *Brevity:* Brevity in storytelling holds attention. Before you speak, ask yourself how much auxiliary information is needed to communicate your message. While this may sound simple, "Brevity is an art."[21] Practice shaving off the fat. It is well worth the effort. Our thoughts begin with gobs of complexity. It is our continued search to find the marrow of what we are looking to understand and then communicate it that gives way to genius. Einstein knew he truly understood an idea once he was able to communicate it to a six-year-old. Hmmm . . . maybe Twitter is a more intelligent forum than I thought.

As you practice offering your valuable gifts, think to yourself, "How can I make whatever I'm doing (a) transformational, and (b) entertaining?" The best way to help people transform their littleness into greatness is to have fun doing so! When fun happens, guards come down and people are ready to be shaken into their next best self. This formula, altered to match the language your people speak, works in all domains. Doesn't matter if you're the CEO of a paper-making company or the next Tony Robbins. Making what you have to say transformational and entertaining mobilizes people!

Let's explore a few tools for making your communication more playful:

DYNAMISM

Every time you open your mouth, speak to be heard. Too many of us speak like we're talking to ourselves. Don't. Instead, do everything you can to ensure the person you are communicating with stays engaged. Take the time to carefully wrap your communication, like a present. Present yourself. Taking what's inside you and offering it as a gift to others is no easy feat. Using your hands will help.

Just as you would take time to handwrite a letter to a friend more neatly than you would write in your journal, when you open your mouth to speak, seek to connect, to be understood.

As we know, it's difficult to define "charisma." However, when we're around someone who commands our attention, we have no problem pointing to the charisma we see. Part of the challenge to nailing down the It is that there is no one way charisma reveals its fabulous self. Charisma has different flavors.

Some charismatics draw us in through the melted-chocolate quality of their voices, soothing our tired souls with their depth of comfort and peace. Even in a roomful of people, we feel they are speaking directly to us, inviting us into their most intimate moments. As with our favorite pillow, we breathe in their grace and feel every knot of tension dissolve. These are the enchanting charismatics. They embody what I have classified as "blue charisma." Blue charismatics include Marilyn Monroe and Frank Sinatra.

Others flip the comfort coin and grab our attention by keeping us on our toes. Not only do they have something to share, they do so in ways that are emotional, opinionated, rhythmic, energetic, unexpected, colorful, pertinent, surprising, and motivational! I have classified these types as having "red charisma." Think Martin Luther King Jr. and Joan of Arc.

Humans are novelty seekers. We are neophiliacs. It speaks of our species' superpower to innovate, and we praise those who do it well. We give them lots of money and attention. Steve Jobs, Bill Gates, Richard Branson, Lady Gaga, Einstein, and Helen Keller, to name a few. Creative charismatics like these carry "orange charisma."*

"Green charismatics," like Oprah Winfrey, offer empowerment and support, while "Golds," like the Dalai Lama, inspire us with loving-kindness and compassion. We each have all the types in us, while expressing one predominant type.

For more on the charisma types and to take a short quiz to uncover your personal type, visit CharismaCodeBook.com. The more you practice your listening, empathizing, and engagement skills, the more you are able to change your charisma type to provide the "color" that offers the most value to your situation.

Your public (including your kids, your dog, and your sweetheart) craves to be engaged. That's why movies are more popular than the news. One way to keep us with you is to switch between charisma types, that is, switch between connection styles. Ask yourself, "What's needed here? Do these people need some blue enchantment, red courage, orange creativity,

---

* The individuals mentioned are for informational purposes only. They represent no endorsement of any product or idea mentioned by Robin Sol Lieberman.

green support, or gold loving-kindness? Give it to them! Then, just as they feel they know you, switch it up. This gives code-switching a whole new meaning. In linguistics, code-switching occurs when a speaker alternates between different languages or dialects depending on whom he is relating to and the environment he is in. To speak charisma code, *The Charisma Code* suggests you use code-switching often. You may have been enacting a blue, Marilyn Monroe charisma type in one moment and in the next, as your public starts to drift off, zap them with that Martin Luther King red! Keep us here. Do anything. Just make us feel alive, interested, curious, sparked by what's possible, thrilled to find out what's next.

Heed the poet Maya Angelou's astute observation: "People will forget what you said. People will forget what you did. But people will never forget how you made them feel."

Much research has been done on the dynamism of excellent leaders. What we traditionally find in great leaders is a quality of dynamism that combines both warmth and authority. To expand on each of these traits, you might look at warmth as being an expression of kindness, inclusiveness, empathy, and care. Warmth is the receptive side of these dynamic leaders, so often found in gold, blue, and green charisma types. The authority side of dynamic leaders is more action-oriented and demonstrates power, stature, confidence, and direction. This type of charisma is red. Orange and green often carry large amounts of power charisma as well. Your goal, should you choose to grow your leadership prowess, is to be yourself. Truth is, you're more flexible in how you express that Self than you probably realize. So, play with expressing a mixture of both warmth and authority.

MUSICAL COMMUNICATION

Charisma is not a language *without* words, though it can be. It is a language *beyond* words. It's the sound of your voice when you speak; it's your body language. One of the ways to use this language beyond words is to implement your natural, monkey-bred ability to speak with feeling. It will sound a bit like music. Listen for the melody, the rhythm, the cadence. If our monkey cousins are anything to go by, musical communication is the best way to influence others' emotions. Try typing "monkey sounds" in the search bar on YouTube and listen to those guys scream, laugh, and "eee . . . eeee . . . eeee . . . ooooo . . . ooooo . . . ooooo . . . oooo." If their exasperatingly direct, melody-rich, sometimes guttural and sometimes shrill sounds don't make you perk up with feeling, I'm not sure you're human! Words alone, coded with information but backed by no emotion, can never match the level of soulful engagement that musical communication inspires. Pay attention to how you use your words, whether you're in your boss's office in a business suit or on your honey's front doorstep with a dozen dandelions. When you open your mouth to connect, let your ready-to-be-unleashed feeling express itself in a wide field of rhythm, cadence, and melodic tones.

Want to practice? Great! Here's an exercise: First, find an environment (actual or virtual) where many people are speaking in a language you do not understand. In a cosmopolitan city this is easy. If you're in a more remote area, Google a foreign movie or YouTube video. Now listen. Notice that when you can't codify the meanings of the words they're using, their voices sound musical. Next, listen to the way you normally speak, using a recording device if you can. Explore the ways you can enhance your speech by adding pauses and volume changes. Discover the melodic spectrum that originates from deep in the low authority of your belly or the high excitement of your head. Once you explore the full dynamic range of your vocal capacity, begin to explore what the real You might sound like. This is where the paths of becoming a charismatic speaker and becoming an enlightened master begin to merge. Oh, wait. They've been together all along—they've been with you through every page of this book.

"Hello, burgeoning charismatic speaker."

"Why, hello there, nearly enlightened master."

"Do you have any guidance for me, nearly enlightened master?"

"Yes, I do. It's important to me that you feel before you speak . . . or don't speak . . . or move a hand . . . or take a step. Your words are ways for who you really are to come out and land in the laps of others. Don't try to entertain. What you may not yet realize in your burgeoning charismatic state is that there is nothing more captivating to another human being than allowing yourself to convey what is really going on inside you."

"Right," replies the burgeoning charismatic speaker. "But sometimes I can't feel anything. My words are like deer frozen in the headlights. How can I make them charismatic?"

"Speak frozen then," says the nearly enlightened master. "Simply feel that they are frozen. If you do that, in time, as with all things, your words will melt and you will feel the symphonies upon symphonies that your soul has been dying to play through you for eons."

FEEL FIRST

Let's go a little deeper into the concept of "feel before you speak." True charisma starts from the heart. Before you open your mouth, remember that a language beyond words is already speaking through you. If you think you should say something, remember that words will not move your listeners to make miracles; only true charisma does that.

So, like jazz, wait for It to come before you open your mouth to spout. Feel before you speak. Once feeling is coursing through your body, whatever you say or do will be magnetic. If saying something you think you're supposed to say was a piece of fruit, it would be a dry, old, wrinkly apple. Saying something you feel wildly alive about would be a ripe, wet mango. Which piece of fruit will you serve?

Here are three ways to grow your ability to speak from wet-mango-feeling instead of dried-apple-supposed-to:

- Imagine you are a large sail, and everything going on around you is the wind. Allow yourself to be moved by that wind . . . and see where you go.

- Breathe and stretch into any constrictions you find in your physical body. This will loosen up stuck emotions, letting them flow through you to power your communication.

- Engage with those who are lit up by passion. Find a way to contribute. Play with them. You become what you relate to.

ADVANCED CHARISMA CODE

There's a step between feeling and speaking that has the power to take your communication from good to great. Send pictures. When you feel something, often the next natural communication step is to see what you are feeling. This step may be subtle and mostly unconscious; however, the best communicators see (and sometimes hear) what they want to transmit. If you feel a deep upset and tightening in your chest, before talking about it, you may see your chest tighten or even associate it with a lemon being squeezed by a lemon press. Speaking this visual metaphor out loud will greatly serve your ability to bring people into your experience. The best communicators string together words, tones, and body language to depict their experience—not an idea of what they should be experiencing or what they wish they were experiencing. That is actually lying—although many cultures do it all the time. Think talking heads. It's hard to believe them or remember a thing they said. The thing is, these talking heads hardly know that what they are saying is out of congruence with their feelings, because they don't know what they're feeling! You can't tell your truth unless you can feel your truth. Otherwise, what's truth? Something someone or some book told you? I don't think so. Others' words and lessons and perspectives don't become ours until we feel them in our bodies and run them through the pattern-making machine in our heads, affirming or denying their validity to us. For truly charismatic communication, feel, see, and then be the message you're trying to send! Your body language will change as you embody your message. Your voice quality will change as you embody your message. Your pauses will change. And yes, even your words will change when you are the message you are trying to send. Feel first. See second. Send third. In time, these steps will dissolve and you will just be charismatic, period.

BODY LANGUAGE

I met Paradox Pollack on March 19, 2011. He responded to a post I wrote on Facebook. It was a question presented by author Ariel Spilsbury: "How high is your ecstasy quotient? Does it need a little cultivation? It's a delight-filled curriculum!"

Paradox's comment: "The realm of Delight is over arched by Delirium in these times. I am cultivating the difference . . . . Btw, you move me."

To be quite honest, I didn't know what this Paradox guy meant, but I liked the image his words provoked in my over-worked, delirious brain; I saw my computer getting machine-gunned down while my ecstasy quotient arched. Yeah. *That.*

When Paradox and I got together a few days later, we began "cultivating the difference." We met along the infamous Star Walk on Hollywood Boulevard. In no time, I surrendered Robin, the work-burdened young woman, and transformed her into a Western damsel with a chivalrous cowboy by her side. We was Billys, talkin' bout "the sweetest peaches dat dun ever been growed." In the next beat, I was Marilyn Monroe and he, Mr. President, secretly courting in the dark and wild Los Angeles night.

Paradox works as one of Hollywood's movement directors. He taught Chris Hemsworth how to swing his hammer in *Thor* and later directed me swinging my whip as Catwoman in film series and stunt shows (but that's another story). If anyone knows about charisma, it's Paradox. A street kid from Philly, he left home at fifteen. He learned how to use the currency of connection to survive. Paradox will tell you that charisma has only one purpose: it brings us all up to eye level.

Paradox spent a year in Bali, Indonesia, learning the intricacies of a ritual called the Kecak, or "Monkey Chant." I saw the ritual performed many times during my anthropological studies in the tiny, plumeria-scented Balinese ocean town of Uluwatu. So, within a month of our first meeting, Paradox and I began leading American and Mexican Monkey Chant groups. We spoke no more than ten different words during the entire hour-long ritual. Instead, we organized hundreds of people into concentric circles, using simple "clown technology." We used this same technique to divide the group into sections and teach them four to six overlapping rhythms. I repeat: we did all of this with no more than ten words.

In America (and all other places not Bali) the Kecak isn't something you run into every day, so most of the people who participated had never seen or heard these rhythms or movements. Still, everyone got it and joined the musical superorganism we clowned into being.

So what is "clown technology"? It's a way of communicating to others, through gesticulations, facial expressions, large body movements, and a cornucopia of emotive primal sounds like "hmmmm, ohhhhh, ahhhh, weeee, ugh, ugh, ugh, no! yesssss!" You've used clown technology before, most likely to communicate with preverbal children and animals.

The greatest gift of clown communication is that it bypasses virtually all word-based misconceptions, of which there are many!

As I'm sure you are more than aware, word language is both a blessing and a curse. My version of utopia would include far fewer words and a lot more clowning. Words are a gift when language facilitates our ability to get inside another person, to know and experience their perceptions, feelings, wants, and dreams. They are a curse when we misinterpret what the speaker means to say.

Do you remember how I asked you at the beginning of this chapter if you or your company have ever felt misunderstood? Of course you have. We all have. Getting good at communicating with emotive, primal language such as clown technology will help you be known for who you really are. It will help others *see your value.*

Try this: Employ clown technology using scale in unexpected ways. Give someone flowers, but instead of the traditional dozen roses, give them a single miniature rose the size of your fingernail. Then, without saying a recognizable word, find another way to "tell" your receiver to put your little flower gift in water. They will laugh, and they will love you all the more for making them laugh.

THE POWER OF THE UNSPOKEN WORD

Comedian Charlie Chaplin's first talkie was *The Great Dictator*; he wrote, produced, scored, directed, and starred in it. This media milestone sparked suspicion in FBI Chief J. Edgar Hoover and the House Un-American Activities Council, who believed that Mr. Chaplin was injecting communist propaganda into the film. Chaplin's career was seriously affected. Once he used words, he became a target for misunderstanding, and "a man with an opinion that is not like mine." Much of the world shunned him and questioned him. They wanted a brilliantly expressive Chaplin—with no voice.

Does that mean you should avoid speaking? No! Just know that on occasion you will be misunderstood. This is the nature of the word-beast. Heighten your chances of being understood by dressing your words with the language beyond words.

Try this: Pause. Charismatic people pause. Allow the pause to add emphasis to your words and actions. Pausing is part of your musical-emotional communication tool kit. A pause invites your listener to come to you. It is by far one of the most magnetic communication tools available. When you have a powerful point to make, nothing makes it better than a pause. You don't have to fill the space. Let the space fill you. If you let it, the space will inform you with the next, most genius thing to do. As a friend of mine likes to say, "Don't just do something; sit there." *Play jazz with your environment.*

Why doesn't everyone use meaningful silence when speaking? One of the most magnetic, captivating, and heartfelt performers I have ever met, magician Eugene Burger, says, "Pausing requires courage." To pause, you must believe that what you have said is worthy of your audience's anticipation. *Know your value.*

GET THEM IN THEIR BODIES

Yes, yes, I know—if they're in front of you they're probably in a body. Thing is, Western culture has cultivated us to pay attention to our thoughts more than our unpredictable (and often uncontrollable), gross, and sometimes blatantly sexy, bodies. If you, as a charismatic, can take us from the rather dull domain of our mind-domes and plant us in the full-on experience of our earthly bodies, we will keep inviting you back, saying, "That was so much fun, we must do it again!"

Get us moving, shaking. Put on music and let us thump to the bass. Maybe even provide burning-hot and freezing-cold pools for us to plunge into. How about hugs? Or breathing exercises to hip-hop genius Tupac?

PROPS

Your charisma tool kit, in addition to the inner and experiential tools, can also benefit from a few tangibles. Carrying charisma props is one way to help bring your charisma power into the physical. Don't worry; your props will come to you naturally, just like everything else genuinely charismatic about you.

As an example, I will share with you the three charisma props that are almost always with me. Each one came my way by necessity.

- *My African basket*: I'm a water drinker. Because they didn't fit in my purse, my big bottles of water were separate, forgettable items I had to lug around. I hated that. One day at a farmer's market, I saw a collection of beautifully woven baskets from Senegal and Nigeria and bought two. These baskets fit my water, my purse, and anything else I want to carry. When I do interviews at a live event, my baskets fit my day camera and sound gear. Added plus: No one steals a basket. If I really want to be safe, I cover its contents with a red velvet cloth. At events, people ask me if I'm selling cookies. Some folks think I'm carrying my cat. If I go to the grocery store, instead of wasting a murdered tree for my groceries, I use my baskets. The checkout clerks usually comment on it, being the coolest bag they've ever seen. I take it to kickboxing and jiujitsu classes at my UFC Gym. The image of wrapped fighter hands carrying a ladies' accessory is hot. The juxtaposition of sweat, fight gear, and the way I carry my feminine basket feels more expressive of my essence than any words I could speak. Nonverbals are a charismatic's best friend. Dynamic nonverbals are a charismatic's secret weapon.

- *My vodka water bottle*: My other two charisma props live inside my basket. The first one, my "vodka water bottle," isn't actually a vodka bottle, but it looks so much like one that everyone laughs when they see me chugging it. "Is that a vodka bottle?" I don't always bring my basket to business meetings, but I always bring my vodka water bottle, because I like how it lightens the mood. I bought my first one at my local health food store for just over two bucks, because I like to drink out of glass, not plastic. It never dawned on me that it shared a close resemblance to the famous potato-liquor packaging. Who doesn't love (or, at least, isn't interested in) a girl who swigs a whole bottle of "vodka" after working out or a woman making business deals while taking a sip from her healthy glass "vodka" bottle now and again?

- *My man bag*: Purchased as a one-of-a-kind item from a Renaissance art faire, my man bag is a male-esque face molded from leather into the surface of my purse. He lives in my basket most of the time. When I take him out for a walk on his own, people go, "Oh, my gosh, her bag's got a face on it! . . . He's looking right at me." I turn to them, smile, and say, "He gets more attention than I do." They like that.

Know what you are facilitating with your charisma props:

- You are providing an opportunity for people to make a connection with you.
- You are using your charismatic ability to evoke feeling in other people.
- You are practicing the charisma fact: Not Everyone is Going to Like You.

Be original in the way you communicate. Seek less-trodden paths. Crowds are tiresome anyway. Find the empty places that don't require competition to survive. Remember, there is no one else like you. So listen for the pathways of communication you are attracted to and use them. If you like calligraphy, send your mate a hand-penned letter with rose petals from your garden, scented with your perfume. If you love to paint, leave hand-painted thank-you notes in the employee lounge. You will be appreciated more than you know.

When looking to use charisma, remember it is an elusive spirit thing requiring form to express itself. Package your charisma in a way that says who you are. If you're trying to get a publisher or production company to buy into your pitch, try sending a bow-tied pitch package with a unique, tangible gift inside. The more senses you engage, the more connected you will become.

Which brings us to emails.

WHY TO ABSTAIN FROM EMAILS AND TEXT MESSAGING

It is of extreme importance that we learn how to communicate. It makes the difference between time spent in little, stupid, avoidable dramas that ramp up to ugly messes, and time spent being understood and collaborating like the fabulous superorganism society member we are biologically designed to be. Through my experience with many types of people, one of the types I have had the opportunity to study in depth is the fifty-something executive male. All of them, adept at doing deals and moving fast, have one communication trait in common: They do not waste time trying to explain things using email. They pick up the phone and call!

When email first became part of mainstream communication, a dear friend and master communicator, Michael Wall, gave me some excellent counsel:

"Email is the devil."

When we email or text, intonations, rhythm, pitch, melody, and body language are not communicated. It is so easy to misunderstand what someone is saying. We can't tell if the other person is a scam artist or an online blessing. Empathizing is nearly impossible; we cannot hear or see our communication partner.

LEVELS OF TRANSPARENCY FROM MOST TO LEAST INFORMATION-RICH MEDIUM OF COMMUNICATION*

1. In person
2. Video or Skype
3. Radio or phone
4. Handwritten letters and packages
5. Social media** and email
6. Wild card: text messaging

Remember that building lines of communication requires that you establish trust. Want to build a following? Show people who you are. Be generous in revealing yourself. By sharing your imperfections openly and honestly, you remind us it's okay to be human. You give us a golden ticket into exploring, rather than rejecting, our own humanity. When trying to decide which medium to use to call your following to you, ask yourself, which medium reveals me the most? Imagine what the world would be like if all governmental agencies practiced full disclosure. Right? You get it. Trust is built on transparency.

BREAK PATTERNS

Pattern breaking is an important part of the charismatic communicator's tool kit. Identify your personal patterns (ruts),

---

* This is a generalization. It is ultimately far less about the medium of communication and far more about the intimacy you conjure through the use of the medium.
** Depending on the use, social media and email are equal in levels of transparency. In social media you give people the ability to see your friends, your history, your boss, and all visual aids giving proof to your being what you say you are ... or not. Email, however, has become more and more intimate, as it is not a given that someone will just hand over their email address. To show up in someone's "primary" inbox means they've already trusted you enough to let you in a little closer. If this understanding is leveraged, emails can be a wonderful way to deepen connection. But remember, if you ever start to see horns and a red trident, pick up the phone!

then break them. You'll maintain an element of surprise in your communications. When in doubt, refer to the earlier section on dynamism and simply intend to change your "charisma color."

Once your listeners can identify a pattern in what you're saying or how you're saying it, they start to zone out, because their pattern-decoding brains have done their "job." This is where your musical communication, clowning, and charisma-type palette come in handy. Change rhythm. Change pitch. Change volume. Change anything! Draw people into the present, where they are aching to be, by catching them by surprise.

Regularly enact your own circumstantially appropriate version of the following Zen story:

> A student comes to his master and says, "Master, I am not progressing in my meditation. Can you help me?" The master looks directly at his student, picks him up by his shirt and throws him out the multi-storied window. During the fall, the student becomes enlightened.

Often, it requires a real shaking up for life to reset to its most beneficial rhythms.

The life stories of Joan of Arc, Galileo, Harriet Tubman, Dr. Martin Luther King, and Malala show us that nothing is more powerful than a movement in opposition to the consensus of the times. That is what revolutions are. They catch the status quo by surprise, and inspire reaction. Sometimes deadly, but always in the direction of progress.

Shake us up! We may complain or fight you at first, but ultimately we love you for it. You provoke us to stretch. If you want to shake us up in ways that make you less likely to get killed, then see no one as your enemy, and seek to speak our "language." I believe it goes without saying there is one universal language we may each be able to get behind; it's called love. When you *see others' value*, it will be hard for them to miss yours.

FLEETING CHARISMA VS. LASTING CHARISMA

What a conqueror!—a conqueror who controls humanity at will, and wins to himself not only one nation, but the whole human race. What a marvel! He attaches to himself the human soul with all its energies. And how? By a miracle which surpasses all others. He claims the love of men—that is to say, the most difficult thing in the world to obtain; that which the wisest of men cannot force from his truest friend, that which no father can compel from his children, no wife from her husband, no brother from his brother—the heart. He claims it; he requires it absolutely and undividedly, and he obtains it instantly.

Alexander, Caesar, Hannibal, Louis XIV strove in vain to secure this. They conquered the world, yet they had not a single friend, or at all events, they have none any more. Christ speaks, however, and from that moment all generations belong to him . . . Now that I languish here at St Helena, chained upon this rock, who fights, who conquers empires for me? Who still even thinks of me? Who interests himself for me in Europe? Who has remained true to me? That is the fate of all great men. It was the fate of Alexander and Caesar, as it is my own. We are forgotten, and the names of the mightiest conquerors and most illustrious emperors are soon only the subject of a schoolboy's talks. Our exploits come under the rod of a pedantic schoolmaster, who praises or condemns us as he likes. What an abyss exists between my profound misery and the eternal reign of Christ, who is preached, loved, and worshipped, and live on throughout the entire world. Is this to die? Is it not rather to live eternally? The death of Christ! It is the death of a God.[22]

Napoléon Bonaparte wrote the above during his final days of confinement by the British on the island of St. Helena. It took conquering most of Europe, then losing everything, for him to realize an important distinction: there is more than one kind of charisma.

Napoleon used fleeting charisma. In fleeting charisma, you look to conquer an audience or win a following.

Christ used lasting charisma. In lasting charisma, you look to give people an experience of their greatness; an experience of their *value*.

In lasting charisma you offer real charity. *Charity*, which shares the same Greek word origin as *charisma*, is gifted when you *see* the Great in people even when they're hiding it under cloaks of self-doubt and self-hatred. You have a choice: you can either explode fleeting charisma in a short spurt, as a parasite, sucking and taking, growing only to burn out; or, if you give to live, you can maintain a sustainable glow of lasting charisma, existing via symbiosis as a conductor of love, joy, and your thrill for life!

Out in the wild, some of earth's oldest species and greatest collaborators, the fungi, join to create an underground network. This shared underground network is called mycelium. Mycelium threads act as a kind of underground internet, linking the roots of different plants, allowing them to share information and nutrients, moving the nutrients between trees and plants to where they are most needed. The "haves" give to the "have-nots," because it pays everyone in the long run. Plants give the fungi nutrition in the form of carbohydrates, and the fungi give the plants a stronger immune system, help them suck up water and nutrients, and connect them to other plants. It's a symbiotic relationship. These mycelial fungi, so much a superorganism that they are almost *beyond* superorganism, support the ecosystem around them, because it is that same system that supports their own life.

Humans give lip service to this and consciously act on it on occasion, but as of the writing of this book, the eighty-five richest people on the planet have as much money as half the world's population of over seven billion. This is a truly sad reality in the face of prevalent hunger and homelessness. We have a genuine global dilemma.

If we look at the way our handful of "haves" hoard in the face of the millions of "have-nots," we might consider adopting the fungi as our mentors in this arena to support our own life. The fungi give to live. They know no other way. And survive they do! They are some of earth's most adaptive species. First appearing 500 million years ago (compared with humans, who've been kickin' our feet for a mere 200,000 years), the fungi have outlived the dinosaurs!

THE FUNGUS-JESUS CONNECTION

Lasting charisma spreads the resource of attention to where it is needed. It *gives* to *live*. When lasting charisma arrives at a party, it looks to see where it can add value and then gives it. When lasting charisma is putting together a marketing campaign, it looks to see what makes its audience feel valuable and creates a story to provide that value. When it shows up at a speaking gig, charisma cues off John F. Kennedy's inspirational call to action: instead of asking what the audience can do for it, it asks what it can do for the audience.

Napoleon's final wisdom on the island of St. Helena shows us that, while he may have been the master of coercion through fleeting charisma, he knew he did not have the lasting charisma of Christ, because he did not "give to live." When you give people an experience of their value, you live in their hearts forever. You can do just that. I see no reason why the future of charisma cannot house seven or eight billion unique Jesuses.

In my role on the global advisory boards of IMPACT Leadership 21 and Alliance 4 Empowerment, I get to work with inspiring and powerful leaders committed to a vision of a sustainable global economy. By helping provide education, technology, and jobs to women, immigrants, and the disenfranchised, we help everyone engage in their local economy. Good for them, and good for their families, right? Right. Yet there's something even greater this economic engagement creates—are you ready for it? Helping people contribute their skills does not just help them make a living; it helps the entire economy! Here's a great statistic from the Bill and Melinda Gates Foundation's 2015 Annual Letter: "By 2030, if women's level of employment in India and Africa rose to match men's, their gross domestic product (GDP) would go up 12 percent."

In order for humans to mimic the fungi in their awesome give-to-live survival strategy, we must create opportunities for people who are currently dissuaded from participating in their local economies the chance to fearlessly gift their gifts.

THE POWER OF INCLUSION

I've been pondering the idea that peace begins with inclusion.

DR. JOSHUA LEVIN, PROFESSOR OF ANTHROPOLOGY

Providing opportunities for others to gift their gifts has a name: It's called being inclusive. It's important for any global leader to know how to wield this powerful tool and to understand why it's so gosh-darn powerful. Luckily, Catalyst is ready to be our schoolmarm:

Catalyst, one of the leading research and strategy development organizations around, is an incredible resource for gathering knowledge on gender, leadership, and inclusive global talent. They recently asked the question, what separates a great leader from a mediocre one? According to Catalyst's 2015 global report called "Inclusive Leadership: The View from Six Countries," it's the ability to lead with an inclusive mindset. Findings in all six countries include the following:

- The more included employees felt, the more innovative they reported being in their jobs.

- The more included employees felt, the more they reported engaging in team citizenship behaviors—going above and beyond the "call of duty" to help other team members and meet workgroup objectives.

- Perceiving similarities with coworkers engendered a feeling of belongingness while perceiving differences led to feelings of uniqueness.[23]

These outcomes obviously boost overall organizational performance. That's nice. So who are you in this story? Are you the inclusive leader or the mediocre one?

You can get a fairly accurate answer by responding to one question—the same question *The Charisma Code* has been asking in various ways throughout these pages. Here it is: Do you make your people feel valued for the unique talents and perspectives they bring to the table . . . or not? Your answer will also be an indicator of which kind of charisma you are currently cultivating—fleeting or lasting.

GIVE TO LIVE

*The open secret here is that if you come to your relationships solely to express the love you **are** by serving another —it is the one certain way to secure your own happiness.*

REV. FA JUN, BUDDHIST PRIEST

Sometimes, we hurt so badly that reaching out to help someone see their value does not feel possible. The last thing we want to do is ask how we can serve another. We become the hoarding villagers in the Stone Soup collaboration story from the beginning of this book, thinking, *I've got nothing. I'm empty and dead inside. I can't possibly give to anyone. I need all I've got just to survive.* But, as Stone Soup shows, when we take the risk of giving the little we have, famine becomes feast, and death becomes life.

Time to put your cozies on and heat your hot chocolate! It's TrueCharisma story-time, with Julie Woods, the Urban Bliss Shaman. Julie told me the following story when I was having a really hard time, and it told me what I needed to know. I hope it will do the same for you or someone you know:

> I was 19 years old in 1979. AIDS was just showing up, wiping out massive quantities of the gay male community. It was wiping away my closest friends. I was watching people get sick and die really quickly. I was in a horrific place; out of work, and I needed something to get me out of suicidal depression. I didn't know what to do to make it easier for me to stay on the planet.
>
> I got down to basics. I love flowers. I love giving flowers. Not so much getting them, but I absolutely adore giving them. And I'm a rose freak. There's a wonderful little shop called Brattle Square Florist in Harvard Square. The florist would let me have a dozen gorgeous roses with little flaws for nothing more than a buck. And I would stand in Harvard Square, surrounded by summertime acoustic music, and give away roses. I'd say, "Please take this rose." People stopped. They wanted to give me money.
>
> "I don't want any money, I just want you to take the flower."
>
> They'd look at me like I was cross-eyed. "Look, I'm having a really shitty day and I will just feel better if you take this flower and go have a great day."
>
> They would laugh. Many would take it, and lots walked away smiling. Some people walked away and looked back to see if I still meant it.
>
> By the ninth flower I felt great. Fantastic [laughing]. Essentially I was creating my own joy by giving to others what I didn't yet have, myself.

I look back and think, *I got that right. I set myself up for joy, and I set other people up for joy.* Now it's a point of honor for me when I meet people, to get them to smile, to have them feel welcome for a moment, in a world that sees them as valuable—that they matter. Whether it's the person at Burger King, or my doctor. If there's a human being in front of me, I want to love on them in a way so that they feel empowered getting to their own joy and bliss.

I get to contribute to that.

When you empower, your Power grows.

MAKE MORE LIFE WITH YOUR LIFE

I'd like to tell you the most catalytic dream I had during my charisma-decoding hermitage. Because of this dream, my engineer-dad was quarantined at the beach with me for days on end, doing his level best to answer my firing squad of questions. I was trying to understand how the universe works through electric circuit theory. At the end of this mind bashing, he turned to me and kindly said the following: "Robin, electric circuit theory is hard. People go to school for years to learn this stuff. I really don't think using hard science will work as a metaphor for teaching people to be charismatic. Have you considered the social sciences?"

THE DREAM

A figure with a powerful presence pointed to the model I was creating of charisma, and told me the answer to the Charisma Code was electrostatic pressure.

When I awoke, I quickly wrote down what I thought were three words: "electro static pressure." I had never heard or, to my knowledge, seen "electrostatic pressure" written before. I had absolutely no idea what the dream meant. I immediately inquired at the Institute of Heartmath, writing to my friend Dr. Rollin McCraty, a scientist who I felt might have a sense of how my dream could be an answer to the Code. Rollin responded with the following:

> Hi Robin,
>
> Electrostatic pressure is a decent metaphor for your work with charisma. An example of electrostatic pressure is the static shock you can get when touching a doorknob after walking across carpet on a dry day. You have accumulated excess electrons from the carpet and the excess electrons jump off of you and onto the doorknob.
>
> Of course in a charismatic individual there are factors that many have written about, personality, etc., but what your intuition is hinting at (and what I told you) is the more important energetic level aspects and the communication and influence that occur at a much deeper level.
>
> Take care,
>
> Rollin

That's right. I'm not teaching you how to shake a hand or how long to hold it. I am teaching you to put a little spark into the hand you're holding! When you become passionately and vitally filled with It, those at a lower energy state (if they allow themselves to be influenced by you) get "sparked to life" as excess charisma "electrons" jump off you and into them. Think about the last time you went to see a charismatic speaker or a singer you love. Their life gave you more life, didn't it? You left feeling more alive than when you arrived, right?

In the electrostatic pressure metaphor, you, as the charismatic, become a transmitter of the holy It. With every spark of charisma you transmit through connection, you uplift and increase others' total energy, and guess what? Your energy does not diminish from this gift; it increases. It's like Julie and her roses in the previous story; when Julie gave her flowers she began to feel full of power. Another way of understanding this $1 + 1 = 3$ logic is remembering a time when you passionately shared an idea with another. Did you feel depleted after sharing your idea or did you discover that once you communicated your thought, more ideas came flooding in?

Why do you think so many people want to be stars? It's not simply to fulfill their human desire to be important. Being a star is a sought-after career because a star gets paid to become a large, living generator of energy. That sh——t is fun! Human stars really do release light like the sun! They are addicted to working the miracle of connecting to their fans (or stakeholders) and releasing "excess electrons" in a blast of light!

SPENDING THE CURRENCY OF CONNECTION IS A 1 +1 = 3 KIND OF A GAME.

In sum, electrostatic pressure is a great supporting metaphor for a key Charisma Code concept: To quote Paradox Pollack one more time, "The true purpose of charisma is to bring everyone up to eye level." When someone becomes radiant with It, their excess "electrons" naturally find their way to those who need a little more charge. They don't need to try. Through the magic of connection, charisma becomes a vitality contagion.

Wish you weren't so tired? Connect to someone or something in such a way that you feel *khárisma, mana, baraka, qi,* It—run through your system, filling you up like excess electrons on a dry day. Energy-producing connection is as simple as seeing the value in whatever you choose to connect with. The energy-producing action of rubbing your feet on dry carpet is akin to the energy you will cultivate when you choose to deeply listen and engage with someone or something. You can use this vitality-enhancement practice to uplift your mood. Anytime you do, you will simultaneously be uplifting the world!

THERE ARE NO PRIVATE THOUGHTS

Remember back in "Step Two: Magnetism," when we talked about growing your own holy halo? Well, what if I told you that there is a very real field of light around you, exchanging information with others? No joke. All life forms have an electromagnetic field around them. Some call this field your "biofield." I call it your halo.

Your halo, or biofield, has an electromagnetic component to it and carries the information of your thoughts and feelings. It's kind of like a full-body, auric mood ring. The different colored halos circling our five charisma types* illustrate this biofield in many of its moods. Scientists know these biofields are there by measuring the effect of the field's force as well as its biophotonic emissions.

What are biophotons?

In 1970, while researching a cure for cancer, physicist Fritz-Albert Popp stumbled on the fact that all living things, from single-celled plants to human beings, emit a tiny current of photons, or light, which he labeled, "biophoton emissions."

The implications for his breakthrough finding became even more exciting when he discovered that the emitted light is a way for life forms to engage in constant nonverbal communication! Life forms use these biophoton emissions to instantaneously communicate, not only with different parts of their own bodies, but with other life forms as well. The following is an excerpt from Lynne McTaggart's book *The Bond*, which takes us deeper into the nonverbal communication implications of Popp's biophoton discovery: "[Popp] discovered that individual living things absorb the light emitted from each other and send back wave interference patterns, as though they are having a conversation."[24] You are having nonverbal, photonic conversations and exchanges with your environment right now. There is not a moment that passes when you are not exchanging information. These conver-

* Refer to first page of this book to see the colored halos of the five charisma types.

sations point to an age-old mystic belief: there are no private thoughts. We are silently, electromagnetically, and biophotonically communicating with other life forms around us all the time. Although this may feel like an invasion of privacy and way more responsibility than you'd like to take on, you can also see it as a great relief. You can now take all the energy you've been spending trying to hide your "real thoughts" and "real feelings" and use that energy to generate "real connection" instead. What are your biophotons saying?

Transparency is a charismatic's pot of gold. Once you become honest, brave, and vulnerable enough to speak what you think and feel with complete honesty, people will experience a peaceful congruency between what your mouth says and what your biophoton emissions (and all your other nonverbal indicators) express.

The result? Trust.

What comes with trust? Receptivity to connection.

What comes with connection? Everything.

So get real. *Inspire engagement from the inside out.*

TURN CONFLICT ON ITS HEAD

The Constitution of UNESCO (the United Nations Educational, Scientific and Cultural Organization), signed on November 16, 1945, declares that "since wars begin in the minds of men, it is in the minds of men that the defenses of peace must be constructed." How can we help move UNESCO's noble principles forward? We need to change our communication in times of conflict. The most effective way to do this is to focus our thoughts on *seeing others' value* at the drop of a hat (or a bomb). If you are an advocate for a culture of peace, you need to develop this ability as if life depends on it—because it does. From my perspective, you and I have been spending time together, developing our subtle and not-so-subtle global communication skills, to get to this moment.

Conflict-free, blow-your-mind communication happens when you vigorously believe the people you're with are made of great stuff. Become like a beaver, determined to build a bridge between yourself and the people you're with no matter how big the rapids or how unnerving their personalities. This doesn't mean you let stinky people walk all over you. It means you become a hero for their greatness. When their big bad littleness occludes their greatness, don your armor of vision and save them! You might compassionately call out their fearful behaviors and invite them to roar a courageous roar. You might also encounter a language beyond words working miracles when you happen to see their greatness in the midst of their less-than-graceful behavior, and all of a sudden, without you saying a word, their shenanigans become very, very funny—to both of you! As I've shared in personal examples, I often see fearful behavior magically transform the moment I choose to look for greatness instead of playing "the little game." As the Constitution of UNESCO suggests, peace starts in the minds of men. Start a culture of peace by looking for value everywhere.

Should you choose to navigate your conversations via this kind of vision, you will avoid unnecessary drama, grief, disgust, hatred, and war.

I once took care of a close family member's home after an unexpected trauma forced her to leave. I ended up living in and caring for her home for over three years. I was told by this family member, whom I love and respect greatly, that her neighbors were essentially made of bad stuff. For at least one solid year I hid from my new neighbors, secretly judging them. With time and direct experience I came to know their generosity, their kindness and their good humor. Upon realizing I had wrongly judged them, I was struck with compassion for warring nations who have a hard time dropping the gun . . . generation after generation.

How willing are you to entertain the possibility that the person you think is out to get you is not actually out to get you?

How willing are you to avoid festering assumptions by asking the person you're communicating with probing questions about whatever is rubbing you the wrong way? How willing are you to believe in the idea of "innocent until proven guilty," even when others have told you that someone is guilty and bad? How willing are you to seek to understand before judging?

Scenario A

Girlfriend #1 says to girlfriend #2: Hey, you look great with that new haircut. A total transformation. You're more boyish, more manly.

Girlfriend #2 thinks to herself: *She's saying I look like a man! I look like a man. This haircut is horrible and my friend is rude.* (Girlfriend #2 runs to the bathroom crying.)

Scenario B

Girlfriend #1 says to girlfriend #2: Hey, you look great with that new haircut. A total transformation. You're more boyish, more manly.

Girlfriend #2 thinks to herself: *She thinks I look like a man. I don't want to look like a man. Is that really what she means? I better ask.*

Girlfriend #2 says to girlfriend #1 in a neutral tone: What about this haircut makes me look more manly?

Girlfriend #1 replies to girlfriend #2: It's a sexy-angled chop like Cameron Diaz in *Charlie's Angels*, Sheryl Stone in *American Pie*, and Halle Berry in *X-Men*. It's absolutely powerful on you!

Girlfriend #2: I don't think of any of those divas as manly. They're hot!

Girlfriend #1: That's what I'm saying; you look freakin' fabulous with your new haircut! I couldn't think of another descriptor other than "manly" in that moment. (Laughs) Ahh, geez, silly me. My more articulate self says you look powerfully angled like a sharp-shootin' chick!

Oftentimes we interpret what others say in the worst way, because we secretly believe we deserve a whipping. In those instances, go back to step one and engage in the confidence-building practices to remind you of the truth: "You are made of great stuff." If you want connection, if you want joyful intimacy, don't grab onto words that rub wrong. Instead, seek to see beyond them. Get your global citizenship visa by seeking to understand instead of judge. That includes judging yourself. If you see your value, you'll be less defensive, more curious. How much can you soften around your *ready-to-battle* thoughts? How many questions can you ask when you find yourself triggered by what you think the other is saying? Tenaciously, diligently, dedicatedly ask questions until you understand what they really meant when they said that thing that hurt you. Get good at asking questions aimed to uncover your conversation partner's innocence, and you'll never have to separate again.

Here is a short list of further practices you can use to cultivate a culture of connection instead of a culture of separation with your subtle yet impactful nonverbal communication:

- Up against someone who is defensive and want to avoid escalating the pain? Be a vessel for true charisma! How? Change your posture, breathing, and thinking to elicit contentment and confidence instead of anger and fear. Ask *what if* you were the embodiment of true, grace-filled charisma and act *as if* you are. Watch as your body and breath change to allow you to present yourself softly, dropping the other person's defenses.

- If you know you are meeting a difficult person, bless the person and your encounter before entering the room or getting on the call. A true charismatic knows the power that's available to them and calls on It often.

- Fully imagine a lover or crush before you approach a person you're having a hard time with. Get detailed. How do you feel when you're with this lover? Activate your visual and olfactory imagination. Let your body come alive with love and heat for this person. Once you feel your cells gyrating with the yes of love instead of the constriction of disdain, engage with your difficult person. (Addendum: Not currently crushing on anyone? Think of your pet . . . especially if she is furry and friendly and provokes instantaneous feelings of "I freakin' love you!")

- Choose to clarify with questions when what you hear feels like an arrow shooting into you.

- Ask yourself, "Is there really such a thing as bad stuff?" "What banged the big bang anyway?" "Who is this person in front of me?" "Who are they *really*?" Pause . . . and wait to be shown.

- Don't fuss it. Laugh!

DISARMING A SUICIDE BOMBER

French-born Amandine Roche was brought to Afghanistan by the United Nations to help organize elections there. As such, she lived in Kabul, on and off, for thirteen years. At the end of her stay there, the US government hired her to monitor Afghan elections, making sure they included women's participation and were free, fair, and democratic.

I met Amandine after writing my first draft of *The Charisma Code*. Amandine was similar to me in appearance and purpose, and we felt our sisterhood immediately. The story that follows is the story she told me within the first hour of our meeting. Her experience is a present-day confirmation of the Charisma Code's power to transform the world.

It was a dark week leading up to the April 2014 election.

Two of my friends were assassinated in a restaurant. One week before the election, the US ambassador called my bodyguard, telling us to evacuate our guesthouse immediately, because they'd intercepted Taliban conversations planning to bomb it. We were evacuated from Jalalabad to Kabul in a black chopper. On top of that, I was having nightmares of repeated bombings. Though I felt truly frightened, I believed strongly in my job and still felt the need to show up to monitor the election.

On election day, I finally decided to visit a polling station. I put on a bulletproof jacket and went with my bodyguard in an armed vehicle. When I showed up at 6:30 a.m. at the polling station, there were 250 women waiting outside to vote for their new president. Inside the polling center were Afghani female electoral workers preparing their respective roles necessary for the election to take place.

At a certain point, I felt something dark and scary on my left side. When I turned to look, I saw a woman as tall as me (I had never met an Afghan woman as tall as me) with superlarge shoulders and a black scarf wrapped around her head in a way no Afghani woman wears her scarf. Her jacket was too short for her. I asked my bodyguard to check out this "woman."

"Be careful," he said. "This person is pretty intense."

I asked my inner guidance, "Who is this person? I need clarity. Who is this person on my left?" I never would have expected the answer I heard. I was not looking for this answer, but I heard clearly, "A suicide bomber." I jumped and started to run.

I was mid-stride when my inner guidance kicked back on again, "No, no, no. Go back and smile at that person." When I heard those words, I knew without a doubt the voice wasn't my own. The idea of going back to smile at that frightening man was so crazy that I knew it wasn't coming from me. I've trained long and hard to differentiate between my ego's voice, the one that's most interested in my survival, and this higher guidance that's most interested in the collective's survival. The voice in my head was definitely the latter, and I chose to follow it.

I went back. The suicide bomber was standing in the same place I'd left him, arms crossed, waiting for the opening of the polling center. He was still and focused, seemingly waiting for the women to come in so he could bomb them.

I was super scared. I went up to him three times, attempting to smile. Two of those times I got close to his face and backed away with fear. The third time he turned his head and looked at me. To say his eyes frightened me is an understatement. They were terrifying! He seemed to be under the influence of the drugs many suicide bombers use to do the extremely dissociated things they do. His eyes were empty and vacant; I could not find a sentient human in there. For one month after this incident, I woke up at 4 a.m. and saw those haunted eyes.

Yet miraculously, in the beat after our eyes met, courage shot through me, and I did what I heard my inner guidance direct me to do: I kept looking into his eyes, and I began to smile at him. There was a pause. Next thing I knew, he was smiling back at me. I remember thinking, "He has a beautiful smile." His humanness had returned.

In that moment, this person took off the official poll jacket he was wearing and walked out of the poll house. He left. Without saying a word, this man, who I believe was prepared to blow up 250 Afghani women, left the poll house and never came back. Scared for the women waiting outside, I screamed to them in English: "Be careful! She is going to blow!" But nothing happened.

I believe my smile disarmed him. Our connection brought him back to life.

"When I'm connected to you, I feel safe. Doesn't matter if we speak the same tongue or if you've got a gun. If you see that I see you, you'll lay down the gun."

ROBIN SOL LIEBERMAN

SOUL FORCE

We must forever conduct our struggle on the high plane of dignity and discipline. We must not allow our creative protest to degenerate into physical violence. Again and again we must rise to the majestic heights of meeting physical force with soul force.

DR. MARTIN LUTHER KING, JR., FROM HIS
"I HAVE A DREAM" SPEECH

"Soul force," a loose translation of the Sanskrit word *Satyagraha*, tied to the practice of civil resistance, is a concept King adopted from Gandhi. Amandine's story is an example of a woman who used her soul force to create peace in a radically challenging environment. She did not try to kill the suicide bomber; nor did she try to get her bodyguard to push him out of the polling house. She also did not run away. Despite her fear, Amandine listened to her "inner guidance" and let her soul force disarm him with a smile.

Remember back in step one when I shared my story of disarming my cranky old grandpa with laughter, love, and a Cosmo styling session? Tofu and granola aside, this stuff works.

As I delved deeper into the philosophy of Gandhi, my skepticism concerning the power of love gradually diminished, and I came to see for the first time its potency in the area of social reform.

DR. MARTIN LUTHER KING, JR.

Remember a few pages before cranky grandpa, when I introduced charisma as the "currency of connection" and I told you, "We are meant to be charismatic, to share the most authentic and valuable parts of ourselves; to communicate what Greek poet Evangelos Alexandreou called 'the jewelry of the human soul?'" Well, this is it. You can revolutionize human relations with your charisma. The time has come to communicate with your soul's force!

SPEAK FLUENT CHARISMA

Now, back to Napoleon, Christ, and leadership. Let's examine the word "theocracy." Taken literally, "theocracy" means "rule by God or gods" and refers primarily to an internal "rule of the heart." Religious studies professor Dr. Stephen Palmquist warns that the political system we call a theocracy is not a true theocracy at all; it is an ecclesiocracy, a form of rulership Dr. Palmquist considers to be most dangerous.

What's the difference between a theocracy and an ecclesiocracy?

In a true theocracy, the leader is believed to have a direct personal connection with divinity. The theocrat is divinely inspired, and their choices rarely make rational sense to anyone else. However, his or her lasting effect can leave a mark on history that makes the rest of us shake our heads in wondrous disbelief, saying, "How was that possible?" This is how Moses led the Israelites; Muhammad, the early Muslims, Joan of Arc, the French troops and how Amandine Roche disarmed a suicide bomber in Afghanistan.

An ecclesiocracy, on the other hand, is a situation in which the religious leaders control the government but do not claim to have a direct personal connection with divinity. Instead, an ecclesiocratic government's leaders typically rule based on religious beliefs, tenets, and interpretations. Even though these rulers claim to be enacting God's plan, there is little room for the unpredictability and miraculous manifestation that often accompany the divine inspiration found in a theocrat's leadership.

Regardless of name, or history, or misuse, or today's use, the actual meaning of theocracy fits quite well in *The Charisma Code*'s system of thinking. Guiding your life and relationships by the rule of your inspired heart will help you speak the language of charisma fluently.

In the words of Marianne Williamson: "If you want to become a leader, become a follower of the inner light."[25]

The purpose of this book is to help you become the kind of person this world needs, the kind of person we were all born to be: a connected person, an invaluable person. A person the tribe wants to protect, listen to, procreate with, share resources with, and be connected to. Every human is born to experience these things. These lessons are, if anything, a repair manual for a culture that has strayed from its own magnificent biology. When we see that it's in our self-interest to serve others, we do. As we approach a global civilization, serving the whole world is undoubtedly in our interest. Armed with the knowledge of these chapters, you are now ready to reintegrate yourself into your superorganism. Show them how good life can be when you *know your value, show your value,* and *see others' value!* But also, remember to have patience. As you do this work, you will start to see the need for it all around you. Be gentle with your fellow humans. Stay strong if they throw tomatoes at you. Be an example. Muster strength by reviewing your Charisma Facts daily:

#1 - *You Are Going to Die.*

So . . .

#2 - *You Must Gift Your Gifts.*

#3 - *Not Everyone Is Going to Like You.*

Still . . .

#2 - *You Must Gift Your Gifts.*

In the words of Eleanor Roosevelt, "Do what you feel in your heart to be right—for you'll be criticized anyway."

So there you have it. All the tools required of a charismatic superbeing. What will you do with these powers? Whom will you influence? What memes will you create? What will you mimic? With whom will you unify, play jazz, change the world? Who are you? How will you be remembered? These are questions only you can answer, but once you have done the work, the answers will be obvious. Now is the time to start. Of course, by completing this book, you have already begun.

CONCLUSION

To fundamentally tackle the roots of conflict, we need to promote an understanding of our common humanity. We need a culture that upholds human dignity and human life.
UNITED NATIONS SECRETARY-GENERAL BAN KI-MOON

Culture is simply what we believe, consciously and unconsciously, to be the right way of doing things. Culture defines rules and norms using a language beyond words. It marks boundaries, tells us what's possible, and helps us determine what we value. It propels us to carry a gun or lock someone up for carrying a gun. It tells us what certain ways of engaging with others mean. *How long should you shake a hand?* If you listen well enough, you can learn *while* shaking someone's hand how the culture for which that person has chosen to be an ambassador shakes hands. Once you experience their way, you will know what to do next.

First **listen**, then **engage,** then **lead.**

The art of charisma is a dance between being receptive to your environment—to every nuance that's going on around you—and simultaneously trusting your inner light enough to shine your gifts even if they are interpreted as weird by the culture you find yourself in.

But here's the magic: If you really *see* who you are with, they will not be afraid of your weird ways. Being seen feels like being respected, so first, see them. In response, those you are with will be attracted to you instead of afraid. At that point, social biology takes over and cultural genetic mutations occur. You try each other on. When the dance is complete, you take away "moves" from them and they take away "moves" from you. Both cultures change in the wake of connection. Enough change and you've got a revolution.

This work requires open-mindedness; it takes a quality of seeing before judging, allowing-in before blocking-out. It asks you to trust your strength enough to love first.

One final exercise from fourteenth-century Sufi Persian poet Hafiz:

> Admit something: Everyone you see, you say to them, "Love me." Of course you do not do this out loud, otherwise someone would call the cops. Still though, think about this great pull in us to connect. Why not become the one who lives with a full moon in each eye that is always saying, with that sweet moon language, what every other eye in this world is dying to hear?

SEE OTHERS' VALUE.

"Lazarus"

APPLIED CHARISMA
CHARISMA, RECIDIVISM, & REFUGEES

Loneliness and the feeling of being unwanted
is the most terrible poverty.
MOTHER TERESA

The term "recidivism" is often used next to the word "rate" to describe the rate or percentage of prisoners who are readmitted to jail for a repeated criminal offense. Recidivism in the United States is astoundingly high. According to an April 2011 report by the Pew Center on the States, the average recidivism rate for released prisoners in the United States is 43.3 percent.[1]

That statistic tells us that nearly half of all former prisoners become prisoners again! Why? The Urban Institute says this happens due to personal and situation characteristics, including the individual's social environment of peers, family, community, and state-level policies.[2]

Being treated as valueless scumbags in prison can't help the situation any. Remember the Pygmalion and golem effects? Our expectations of others affect performance. And what about the fact that ex-offenders leave prison with the mark of an "ex-con" on their job applications? This is not at all conducive to giving these people a sense of belonging in their new social structures outside prison. It is precisely this attitude of exclusion that often creates the most dangerous felons.

What to do? Well, highlighting rehabilitation vs. punishment in prison is a must. Programs that help prisoners *know their value, show their value,* and *see others' value* are appropriate. Additionally, programs that help prisoners find a sense of belonging in society outside prison walls are necessary. None of these ideas are rocket science, and I am certainly not the only one to be discussing them. I believe the Charisma Code can be applied to any situation in which we are looking to improve the way we relate to one another—especially in those situations when we need to find a way to relate to people we deem different from ourselves.

Lowering recidivism rates by better integrating ex-offenders into mainstream society is similar to the current social issue we face with helping integrate refugees into new countries. Both "mainstream society" and the "new countries" reap benefits when they invite the "outsiders" to contribute. However, if they do not understand the ex-offenders and the refugees, they are likely not to trust them either. The result is more us-versus-them shenanigans instead of reaping the benefits of diversity through inclusion.

Take heed of these wise words as spoken by one of the most articulate geniuses I know and love, anthropologist Dr. Joshua Levin. They point out a path to peace. Dignity for all. Inclusivity a must. Here's Joshua:

> It is at that point, line, wall, behind which people are excluded from co-creation and a common destiny, that the marginalized are forced to choose between accepting their oppression or fighting. If you can't join them, beat them . . . hate them . . . and create an identity that is organized around the indignity and righteousness of your victimization. One must be excluded to be a martyr, and once the ferocity of

oppositional identities become entrenched, it is very difficult to see their origins. It appears as though their hate is the very cause of the exclusion, rather than exclusion the cause of hate. Peace is predicated on identifying with common cause, and common cause is the beginning of inclusion. It is in that space where we can imagine creating a future **together**, that peace between us becomes possible. Once a person or a people is pushed beyond our circle of care, once they become Other, the rules of survival change from cooperation to competition, from compromise to combat. When they become us, and we become them, enmity is recast as solidarity. On one level it's really quite simple, peace comes from a commitment to work together for our mutual benefit. It is the inclusive, "we," the "our," in that last sentence, that is essential. When we are brought together within the circle of care, our differences require us to make as much room as possible for diversity without threatening our shared destiny. The end of peace is the point at which conflicting perspectives find it impossible to compromise and include each other.

CHARISMA &
CLIMATE CHANGE

Now is the time for courageous actions and strategies,
aimed at implementing a "culture of care."

POPE FRANCIS, SPEAKING TO THE
UNITED STATES CONGRESS, 2015

Thirst. Hunger. Fire. Human-created climate change threatens us in a way our species (and so many other species) have never been threatened before.

Revolution, anyone?

We used our whatiferousness to get us into this mess. That same superpower will help us get out. We did not slide into this climate conundrum alone, just as we will not emerge alone. It will take all nations working collaboratively and in solidarity with one another towards the following singular goal: *survival*.

Effective action towards the preservation of diverse life on earth demands we connect to our entire global superorganism species as a means of quickly enacting worldwide, systemic change. We're talking about implementing a renewable energy infrastructure, folks. And fast!

Q: How do we work together towards a grand, global goal like this one when our species does not speak the same language or value the same thing?

A: We can connect and communicate using the language beyond words. We can use soul force. We can use our collective charisma.

Collective charisma is what happens when a collection of inspired and committed individuals join forces towards a passionately desired common goal. It's what impassioned solidarity looks like.

As the literal translation for "corporation" is a group of persons united in one body, the entire human species needs to incorporate in good ol' superorganism fashion for its survival. In the case of *Homo sapiens*, it has always been thus. The only difference today is that instead of working together to hunt local prey, we need to work together to find a new relationship with our prey so that we do not become the earth's prey.

We have been hunting the earth for much too long.

The paths leading away from the dire scientific predictions resulting from global warming do not have to be dreary. Quite the contrary, they are a mandate for us to adapt to the current environmental challenges we face using *The Charisma Code*'s connection-for-action prescription: Listen, Engage, Lead! Warring nations will hop on the same team. There can be no Us against Them on Mission: Save Humanity from Climate Change. Peace comes from a commitment to connect and work together, towards the same goal, for mutual benefit. Putting a stop to climate change is the naked goal sprawled-out on today's global table.

Here's the joy: most things wearing the mark of connection feel good. I'm thinking of baby-making activities. I'm thinking of love. I'm thinking of hugging a dog and punching a bag and dialoguing with a smart person. I'm thinking of parent pride on graduation day, presidential election parties and a refugee family sleeping through the night in their new neighborhood. I'm thinking of ex-offenders selling bouquets of flowers and little boys wanting to grow up like their papas. I'm thinking of bacteria and mitochondria and DNA proteins gyrating in ways invisible to us yet deeply connected to their function within the whole of life. I'm thinking of that slide of lavender soap and weight of foot, footprinting sand. I'm thinking of sand paintings that are erased again and again. I'm thinking of my breath. And your breath and that butterfly flapping its wing in Australia . . .

Diverse humans connecting through the shared goal of staying alive might just be fun. The global communication tools you can use to help enable collective direct action with people different than you are pretty basic: *know your value, show your value, see others' value.* Because an end to climate change requires a type of global inclusivity we are yet to see in the story of *Homo sapiens*, we need to give serious thought to working with people vastly different than ourselves.

We are at a turning point; future generations will look to this crux in time to see how we responded. Did we listen to the icebergs melting? Did we see half of the life in the sea die before our eyes in the short geological blink between 1970 and 2016? Did we do anything about it? Are you? Compassionately *what if* your way to a solution with us. It's what we are made for. Let's use our collective charisma to save ourselves and so much more.

CHARISMA AND
THE ECONOMY

Economically, charisma is more important today than ever before. Beginning with Marco Polo and the Silk Road, today's global trade and connection allow us to get almost anything we want for the bottom dollar. If everyone is selling red slippers for pennies compared to the handmade and local (but pricier) red slippers of our past, then what differentiator other than best price will shoppers use to pick whom they buy their red slippers from? Can you guess?

Those who use the Currency of Connection!*

I recently spent a week at Zappos' headquarters in downtown Las Vegas, studying the famous online shoe store's corporate culture. Zappos is built on the belief and practice that a strong company culture founded on excellent customer service helps create a strong company brand. They are right. Most everyone loves Zappos, even its employees. During my visit, I spoke with Zappos' CEO, Tony Hsieh. I asked, "What quantifiable business metrics** do you have that would tell me, as a business leader, that investing in my company culture is a worthwhile investment?"

He responded with five simple words: "Our employees are more engaged." This was not the quantifiable metric I was looking for, but it did reveal something important that I believe speaks

---

* Obviously, factors like aligned ethics and geographical locale can also act as company differentiators in terms of whom we choose to buy our red slippers from. These are ways of using the currency of connection.
** As defined at www.klipfolio.com, a Business Metric is "a quantifiable measure that is used to track and assess the status of a specific business process." It is a company's foundation for any performance-monitoring strategy.

to the broad implications of *The Charisma Code:* Engagement is what we are after. Companies know it relates to business performance, and we intuitively know it relates to life performance.

> **Charismatic Person:** Someone who's got that "It" about them that people want to engage and connect with.
>
> **Charismatic Company:** A company that's got that "It" about them that customers want to engage and connect with.

We run from boredom like Ebola, fumbling towards engagement. Similarly, we seek to engage others with our ideas and products, our looks and our cars, our smiles and our social media posts. We want to engage the boss we are hopeful will hire us and the kids who might listen to us before crossing the road. We want people to buy *our* red slippers!

Charisma can help with that. Charisma connects and charisma inspires engagement. How? Through a mesmerizing language beyond words called soul force.

The verdict is in. 2,000+ CE is ruled by the connection economy. We now know how to make cheap things. Fine. Do it. Do it ethically. But remember that cheap is only one type of value. Humans, via their superorganism nature, are magnetized to enviornments that provide a sense of connection, a sense of belonging, a sense of feeling great. If money represents value, and charisma is cultivated by knowing and seeing *real value*, then these two coveted representations of value may just be gettin' it on more than we previously realized.

It has taken me most of my life to understand just how important money is to culture. I think culture is the bees knees, the coolest thing since PB and J . . . Oh wait, PB and J was invented and adopted by culture. What I mean to say is that one of the strongest ways cultural paths form is around the flow of money. I imagine money as rocks and culture as a river, changing course to accommodate the rocks. Money is in our politics, in our houses of worship, in our universities, and maybe under your mattress. Money sways opinions. Its flow can make the difference between cultures that dance in the streets and cultures that build fences around their streets. Money is important because, as a global superorganism, we have made it equivalent to value. And value is everything. Just as we protect what we are connected to, we protect what we value. Here's the cool: No separate force or source demands we deem certain things valuable over other things. *We* deem them so. Humans. *Homo sapiens.* Meme makers. Revolution makers. Whatifers. Culture-creators. *We* are the makers of ideas, and thus we are the makers of what we deem valuable and worthy of living for. As beauty is in the eye of the beholder, so is value.

Dream on, my fellow revolutionaries, and please, spend your currency of connection without a worry for tomorrow.

CHARISMA AND GLOBAL CITIZENSHIP

The era of global citizenship is here. It demands we accept three things:

1. **Planet is home**
2. **Nature is guide**
3. **Cross-mingling is natural.**

Let's begin with **planet is home.**

Global citizens do not belong to Cuba, Chicago, or Tibet. Global citizens belong to the Earth. Sure, they may own a home in Cuba, Chicago, or Tibet, but their membership is to the globe. As a citizen of the world, no matter where I own my home, pay my taxes, and grow my plants, what happens in Cuba, Chicago, Tibet, and beyond is my business.

The era of global citizenship demands number two: **Nature is guide**.

From core to surface to atmosphere and all creatures in between, nature is everywhere. Nature is global. You can't leave nature. It's the way of all earthly things—including you. Nature is inclusive of everything that is alive. It does not pick sides, deciding who's right and who's wrong, bad or good. Nature does not judge. It just is. What better guide to lead the emerging culture of global citizenship than nature?

Remember biomimicry? Here's a refresher: Biomimicry is a biological innovation tool that helps humans create spectacular and sustainable innovations by mimicking nature's genius. It's pretty impressive that all things currently existing on Earth show off 3.8 billion years of tried and true survival strategies. What if we could emulate those successful and sustainable strategies when we're looking to design a new political process, healing art form, building, or relationship? We can and it's actually quite simple. Here's how: the next time you're looking to design something new, ask, "What would nature do?" If you ask this question every time you make a decision, express yourself, or create something new to contribute to humanity's superorganism soup, you will be following the era of global citizenship's demand number two: **Nature is guide**.

The leading research, training, and consulting organization in biomimicry, Biomimicry 3.8, has made a system we can use to more easily follow the genius in nature by observing and articulating nature's life principles. These life principles are the actions we see nature demonstrating over and over again. They're the principles nature follows to bloom. These life principles are the literal byproduct of 3.8 billion years of evolution. Here are just a few of these life principles articulated by Biomimicry 3.8:

- Be locally attuned and responsive.
- Adapt to changing conditions.
- Evolve to survive.

And here's how these principles can work for you. When looking to design a charismatic presentation, you can ask, "What would nature do?" Oh, nature would "be locally attuned and responsive." OK, so I will listen and respond to my audience while presenting instead of dishing out a scripted monologue that's disconnected from my audience. Cool. Got it. And if my audience gets really cold during my presentation because the heater is broken, I will "adapt to changing conditions" by turning on some music and leading my fav Zumba dance steps.

As humanity evolves to align itself with nature's intelligence, we not only secure our survival as a species, we more easily connect with anyone, anywhere! Which brings us to the era of global citizenship's third demand: **Cross-mingling is natural.** Whole-world interconnectivity, made technically possible through media, internet, and airplanes, means we are regularly interacting with people who have radically different backgrounds and values than we do. Groovy. But whose language do you speak and what do you do when you disagree?

To me, the hottest thing about the twenty-first century is its mandate to cross-mingle. Because of it, we have an opportunity to either (a) accept "the mandate" and never feel outside the circle of belonging again or (b) separate ourselves from the twenty-first century's cross-mingling and feel like outcasts—cast outside the circle of care. We choose option (a) when we practice *knowing our value*, *showing our value*, and *seeing others' value*. When we choose to cross-mingle, we reap the rewards that come with expanded, diverse networks. We feel the warm satisfaction and expansive safety of feeling at home wherever we go. We get a chance to work together as the enormous superorganism species we are. We rise to the occasion of addressing our global community's crises. We work together to save our asses!

Our desire to survive and thrive
is bigger than our differences.

As we learn to connect with anyone, anywhere we move towards an unprecedented experience of personal and planetary wholeness. We get to enjoy apples *and* oranges. We get to enjoy apples and oranges *and* cherimoyas. The more moments we spend dancing with the various flavors of life, the more passionately engaged we become. The more passionately engaged we become, the more the often mysterious "gift of grace" comes flooding into our lives, transmitting itself to others as the charismatic contagion it is. Similarly, the more flavors any one of us pushes away in disdain or disgust, the less magnetic, appealing, and valuable we become to our fellows. Charisma is the currency of connection. The twenty-first century demands we spend more of it than we are right now.

Question: What will it take to open up the confines of *Homo sapiens'* tribal mind to include the whole world as part of our tribe?

Answer: *Communicating in a language beyond words.* We will code this language with love and we will ask our charisma to secretly transmit It everywhere we go.

EPILOGUE

With all the cracked sidewalks I walked on during my elementary school years, I only ever made one wish; each time I stepped over a crack, I wished to be magic. I know I am not alone in this wish. The wish is there because we know, deep down, that we and others carry a great source of untapped power. Now, as a woman, I no longer read books about telekinesis or turning crystal balls into roses. I do not engage myself in the study of traversing time and space so that I can get to China without a jet plane. I don't seek to blink water into wine or little houses into mansions. With that said, *I still wish to be magic.*

The difference is this: I am now interested in cultivating the deepest and highest magic I have found—the magic that turns suffering into joy, confusion into clarity, isolation into peace, numbness into feeling, hell into heaven. The magic that soothes the little girl when she wakes up in the middle of the night, terrified by the crawling insects on her ceiling. The magic that takes the confusion of conflicting dreams and settles them in the peace of knowing what's real.

I am interested in the magic that gets businessmen dancing again.

Magic is always about transformation:

> The magician transforms the empty hat into hat with rabbit.
> The alchemist transforms lead into gold.
> Jesus transforms one fish into many fish.
> The comedian transforms pain into laughter.
> The shaman transforms sickness into health.
> The diva transforms grey into color.
> The poet transforms the formed into the possible.

Grace is the unexpected transformation, the unexpected magic. But there is more; grace in and of itself is flaccid. It needs hands to work through. When any one of us realizes we have just as many capable hands as anyone else; when the pull to live the life of the Greats pumps through our blood; when all the little dramas and battling confusions, judgments, and comparisons lose their magnetic appeal, we radiate with a new magnetism: a magnetism born of artists' hands dipped in grace paint.

You now have everything you need to paint your world canvas. Although there will still be times when you doubt the masterpiece you paint, the life you live, rest assured you are creating a well, a gift that all the thirsty creatures can gather 'round and drink from.

You are that well. You are what gets filled with the gift of grace. Your soul force is at the ready. Lil' ol' you. Like Jesus, Mohammed, Ghandi, Genghis Khan, Oprah, Darwin, Confucius, Cleopatra, Einstein, Mozart, Marilyn Monroe, Martin Luther King, the Dalai Lama, Malala, Temple Grandin, John Lennon, Joan of Arc, Lucille Ball, Richard Branson, Frida Kahlo, Salvador Dali, Katharine Hepburn, Archbishop Desmond Tutu, Amma, Dorothy Day, P!nk, Beyonce, Buddha, Che Guevara, Rumi, John F. Kennedy, Jim Carrey, Michelangelo, Misty Copeland, Malcom X, Janitor X, Leonardo da Vinci, Charlie Chaplin, Jackie Chan, Nelson Mandela, Will Smith, Robin Williams, Marianne Williamson, Thomas Merton, Aung San Suu Kyi, Jane Goodall, Kahlil Gibran, Harriet Tubman, Abraham Lincoln, Helen Keller, Steven Spielberg, Thich Nhat Hanh, Amy Purdy, Maya Angelou, Pope Francis, Lady Gaga, Steve Jobs, Stephen Hawking, Elvis, Ellen, Galileo, Eckhart Tolle, Anaïs Nin, Princess Di, Mother Teresa, and countless others, you have what it takes. Let's make some magic.

NOTES

Introduction

1. Mark Oppenheimer, "Charm School," *Boston Globe*, 20 July 2008.

Charisma: The Currency of Connection

1. Jane Goodall, cited in Dale Peterson and Mark Befoff, *The Jane Effect: Celebrating Jane Goodall* (San Antonio: Trinity Press, 2015), p. 53.
2. Adam Grant, *Give and Take: A Revolutionary Approach to Success* (New York: Viking, 2013).
3. Brendon Bruchard, *The Charge: Activating the 10 Human Drives that Make You Feel Alive* (New York: Free Press, 2012), p. 1.
4. John Potts, *A History of Charisma* (New York: Palgrave Macmillan, 2009), p. 21.
5. Matthew 7:7.

Step One: Confidence

1. Potts, *A History of Charisma*, p. 5.
2. Tony Robbins, "If I Were 22: Hunger Will Destroy Your Fear of Failure," *LinkedIn Pulse*, May 27, 2014.
3. Albert Einstein, *Out of My Later Years* (New York: Philosophical Library, 1950), p. 260.
4. Stuart L. Brown, "Consequences of Play Deprivation," *Scholarpedia* (2014): doi: 10.4249/scholarpedia.30449.
5. Lisa Furgison, "Study: Younger Men More Apt to Talk About ED," *AccessRx Blog*, February 3, 2014, https://www.accessrx.com/blog/erectile-dysfunction/young-talk-about-ed-l0203/.
6. Alessandra H. Rellini, Katie M. McCall, Patrick K. Randall, and Cindy M. Meston, "The Relationship Between Women's Subjective and Physiological Sexual Arousal," *Psychophysiology* 42 (2005): 116-24.
7. Andrew Newberg and Mark Robert Waldman, *How God Changes Your Brain: Breakthrough Findings from a Leading Neuroscientist* (New York: Ballantine Books, 2009), p. 75.
8. Ibid., pp. 77-9.
9. Ibid., pp. 14-6.
10. Ibid.
11. Robbins, "If I Were 22".

12. In a personal communication to Robert Pope from October 2, 1996, Sagan wrote: "**I am not an atheist**. An atheist is someone who has compelling evidence that there is no Judeo-Christian-Islamic God. I am not that wise, but neither do I consider there to be anything approaching adequate evidence for such a god. Why are you in such a hurry to make up your mind? Why not simply wait until there is compelling evidence?" In Joel Achenback, "Carl Sagan denied being an atheist. So what did he believe?" *Washington Post* (July 10, 2014): https://www.washingtonpost.com/news/achenblog/wp/2014/07/10/carl-sagan-denied-being-an-atheist-so-what-did-he-believe-part-1/

STEP TWO: MAGNETISM

1. Rudyard Kipling, "Mrs. Bathurst," *Kiplingsociety.co.uk* (2010). Originally published in England: *Windsor Magazine* (1904), http://www.kiplingsociety.co.uk/rg_bathurst1.htm.
2. Elinor Glyn, cited in Jeanine Basinger, *Silent Stars* (Hanover, NH: Wesleyan University Press, 199), p. 436.
3. Samantha Sumi Barbas, *Movie Crazy: Fans, Stars, and the Cult of Celebrity, 1910-1950* (Berkeley: University of California Press, 2000), p. 73.
4. Len Sperry, *Handbook of Diagnosis and Treatment of DSM-IV Personality Disorders* (New York: Brunner Routledge, 2003), p. 152.
5. Thom Hartmann, *The Last Hours of Ancient Sunlight: Waking up to Personal and Global Transformation* (New York: Broadway Books, 2004, audio book).
6. Philip Rieff, *Charisma: The Gift of Grace and How it Has Been Taken Away from Us* (New York: Pantheon Books, 2007), p. 239.
7. Dr. Mario Martinez, *The Mind-Body Code: How the Mind Wounds and Heals the Body*, (Boulder: Sounds True, 2009, audio book).
8. Time, "Russell Brand Explains How to Start a Revolution," YouTube, 2:06, October 31, 2014, https://www.youtube.com/watch?v=zIIpNJDC0nw.
9. Marianne Williamson, *A Return to Love: Reflections on the Principles of "A Course in Miracles"* (New York: Harper Collins, 1992), p. 190.
10. Ibid.
11. Max Weber, *Economy and Society*, Guenther Roth and Claus Wittich, trans., (Berkeley: University of California Press, 1978), p. 241.

12. Seth Godin, "Attitude is a Skill," *Seth's Blog*, September 25, 2015, http://sethgodin.typepad.com/seths_blog/2015/09/attitude-is-a-skill.html.

13. Discovery News, "Dogs Automatically Imitate People" (February 11, 2013): http://news.discovery.com/animals/pets-dogs-imitate-people.htm.

14. James Fowler and Nicholas Christakis, "Dynamic Spread of Happiness in a Large Social Network: Longitudinal Analysis Over 20 Years in the Farmingham Heart Study," *BMJ* (2008): doi: http://dx.doi.org/10.1136/bmj.a2338.

15. Amy Cuddy, "Your Body Language shapes Who You Are," *Ted Talks*, June 2012. https://www.ted.com/talks/amy_cuddy_your_body_language_shapes_who_you_are.

16. Michael Lynn, Joseph-Mykal Le, and David S. Sherwyn, "Reach out and Touch Your Customers," *Cornell Hotel and Restaurant Administration Quarerly*, 39:3, (1998): 60-5, http://scholarship.sha.cornell.edu/cgi/viewcontent.cgi?article=1111&context=articles.

17. William Shirer, *Berlin Diary: The Journal of a Foreign Correspondent, 1934-1941*, (Baltimore: John Hopkins University Press, 2002), p. 21.

18. Qur'an, Surah 49:13.

19. Rishi Lyengar and Victor Luckerson, "What We Know So Far About the Oregon Shooter," *Time*, October 2, 2015, http://time.com/4059136/oregon-shooter-ucc-chris-harper-mercer/

20. Dr. Martinez, *The Mind-Body Code*.

21. Neale Donald Walsch, *Conversations with God, Book 2: Living in the World with Honesty, Courage, and Love* (Charlottesville, VA: Hampton Roads, 2012), p. 32.

Step Three: Connection

1. Olivia Fox Cabane cited in Anita Bruzzese, "You Can Develop Your Own Charisma, Author Says," *USA Today*, April 5, 2012.

2. Robert Greene, *Mastery* (New York: Penguin Group, 2013, audio book).

3. Ibid.

4. Dr. Rollin McCraty, e-mail message to author.

5. Ibid.

6. Mark Goulston, *Just Listen*, (New York: Amacom, 2010), p. 48.

7. Ibid.

8. RSA, "Brené Brown on Empathy," YouTube, 2:53, December 10, 2013, https://www.youtube.com/watch?v=1Evwgu369Jw.

9. Ibid.

10. See John Kenneth Galbraith, *The Age of Uncertainty* (Boston: Houghton Mifflin, 1977), p. 330.

11. Don Miguel Ruiz, *The Four Agreements* (San Rafael: Amber-Allen Publishing, 2008), p. 48.

12. Carol Kinsey Goman, *The Silent Language of Leaders: How Body Language Can Help—or Hurt—How You Lead*, Audible Studios (2012): 2:22:35, audio-book.

13. RSA, "RSA Animate: The Power of Outrospection," YouTube, 10:28, December 3, 2012, https://www.youtube comwatch?v=BG46IwVfSu8.

14. Ibid.

15. Ibid.

16. Cited in, *The Federal Career Service: A Look Ahead*, Society for Personnel Administration (1954).

17. Robert Rosenthal and Lenore Jacobson, *Pygmalion in the Classroom: Teacher Expectation and Pupils' Intellectual Development*, (New York: Holt, Rinehart and Winston, 1968).

18. Ronald E. Riggio, "Pygmalion Leadership: the Power of Positive Expectations," *Psychology Today*, April 18, 2009.

19. Mt. 7:12.

20. Ken Keyes, *The Hundredth Monkey: And Other Paradigms of the Paranormal* (New York: Prometheus Books, 1991).

21. Jeff McBride, conversation with the author.

22. Hilarin Felder, *Christ and the Critics: A Defense of the Divinity of Jesus Against the Attacks of Modern Sceptical Criticism, Volume 2*, John Lawson Stoddard, trans., (England: Burns, Oates, and Washbourne, Ltd., 1924), p. 216-17.

23. "Inclusion Matters," *Catalyst*, March 2, 2015, http://www.catalyst.org/knowledge/inclusion-matters.

24. Lynne McTaggart, *The Bond: How to Fix your Falling-Down World* (New York: Free Press, 2011), p. 64.

25. Marianne Williamson, Personal Facebook Post, September 9, 2013.

Applied Charisma

1. Public Safety Performance Project, State of Recidivism: *The Revolving Door of America's Prisons*, The Pew Center on the States (April 2011).

2. Transitions From Prison To Community: *Understanding Individual Pathways*. The Urban Institute, Justice Policy Center, Washington, District of Columbia.

ACKNOWLEDGMENTS

*We only see how far we can go by virtue
of the giants on whose shoulders we stand.*

JIM JITSU

I scale tall shoulders. Shimmy up deltoids, trapezius, and upper cervical spine till I reach the vantage of eyes that know how to see. I sniff out the Great like Cleopatra sniffed out power. Once I find It, I peer through Its eyelids by asking It questions. *The Charisma Code* is my assembly of Its answer.

In the sentiment of Dr. Martin Luther King, those who have chosen to "be creatively maladjusted" in the face of status quo mediocrity are the ones *on whose shoulders we now stand*. Thank you. Without the courage of so many convictions, I would never know how great Great can get. If I did not know that, there would be no reason for me to write *The Charisma Code.*

There are so many giants in my life, I am shy to begin calling out specific names, but I must mention a formative few: Mrs. Benedetto, my second grade teacher, who placed my creative writing paragraph on display, declaring with that action I wasn't as "dumb" as my first grade teachers seemed to want the other kids (and me) to believe. Then in eighth grade, Mrs. Cunningham and Mrs. Meylor awarded me the badge of "Most Likely to be Published," followed by my high school senior class, who voted me "Most Unique." Today I live in these childhood shoes you stitched for me, so grateful I do not walk alone.

The numerous iterations of *The Charisma Code* have been heard, evaluated, diced, digested, questioned, laughed at, offered anew, moved around, smashed, and applauded by *many*. To you I say, *Thank you.* Thank you for letting me charisma-bomb your parties with my questions. Thank you for giving me something to write about every time you showed your value. Thank you for helping me to *see how far we can go* and for telling me how badly you ache to go there. Many of you swooped in at critical moments, offering insights that consequently changed the keys to the Code. That's you, Michael Wall, Jonathan Cardozo, Thalyn Nikolau, Marjorie Hass, Jim Jitsu, Rollin McCraty, Christopher Patton, Joshua Levin, Jeff McBride, Naila Chowdhury, Feroza Ardeshir, Suresh Subramani, Constance J. Peak, Twyla Garrett, Amandine Roche, Kim Hix, Mark and Shannon, James Ruesch, Davie-Blue Bacich, Vida Vierra, Dr. Richard Hansen, Early Reese, Claudia and Shelly, Arnold and David, Sarah Lipton, Penny Olson, Michele Schwartz, Jaiya, Ian Ferguson, Michelle Barton, Kaia Ra, Fa Jun, Marya Stark, Sanjiv Sidhu, Marla and Olaf Hartmann, Armen Orujyan, Ruzanna Avetisyan, Joshua Luber, Wim Hof, Wendy Newman, Starhawk, Roald Marth, and Robert Richman.

A few steadfast souls dared stay connected with me throughout my entire hyper-focused charisma frenzy. When you read your name, I pray you know how much I cherish your brilliance and stand-by-me patience. You are sterling: Julie Woods, Michael Levine, Marc Scarpa, David Shapiro, Stephen Shapiro, Linda Nicholes, Howard Stein, Andreea Petruse, Sue Romatz, Mandy Ward, Steve Lieberman, Victoria Lieberman, and the rest of you Liebermans.

Liberty caps off to my creative team, without whom this book would be mere notes—not music. Sage and Ember Knight, your tireless reading and wise re-forming of *The Charisma Code* have made this work accessible. Although the rearing writer in me wanted to press print long ago, your soul-dripping attention to editorial detail is exactly what the universe ordered. Tamsin Woolley-Barker, your contributions to the Code are beyond the beyond. Besides contributing countless hours of biological dialogue to the backbone of this book, you are my stellar friend and my writing coach. Because of you I am doing my best to eradicate *was doing, had been, that, able to,* and *can be seen* from my vocabulary. You keep me present. I know, in my own way, I do the same for you. To Lieve Maas, for helping me articulate *The Charisma Code* in a visual language beyond words from the get go. Your tireless attention to this evolving project is a major ingredient in this book's Stone Soup. To Christy Collins, Michele Zousmer, Clay Patrick McBride, Mouth Public Relations, Rory McCracken, Thomas O'Brien, Nikki, Starla Fortunato, Melissa Michelle, Vivian Francis, John Rowe, The Tanori Group, Martin Bridge, Kiva Singh, Shannon Lieberman, Patrick Bastien, and Congressman Alan Lowenthal: you have each contributed something of artful necessity to the visual component of *The Charisma Code.* To my hairdresser, Jenna Erin Murray: Thank you for your fearless way with scissors.

To my body team: Laura Stuve, Myriam Machado, Frances Severance, Dana Hirsch, Viver Brasil, and my trainers at the UFC Gym in Yorba Linda—as you all know, I'm not built for computer work; I'm built to dance and to fight! Thank you for keeping my body and soul together through this.

To Paradox Pollack: I hope, after reading this book, you'll understand what I left for.

To Marianne Williamson, a hero of our times: Thank you for *seeing me* and introducing me to *A Course in Miracles*, the text that has most influenced my life and consequently *The Charisma Code.*

To Debbie Lieberman, Commissioner of Montgomery County, and John Theobald for first inviting me to teach *The Charisma Code* in prisons and with ex-offenders. Never have I felt more fulfilled . . .

To Congressman Tim Ryan, thank you for recognizing the Charisma Code as a tool to help create "A Mindful Nation."

To Janet C. Salazar, writer of this book's foreword: Without you, *The Charisma Code* would likely live within the walls of one nation; because of you, it flies as an inked citizen of the world! You are a theocrat. This book and I are grateful you listen and obey!

To Ambassador Anwarul K. Chowdhury—the ultimate global citizen—thank you for supporting me and the message in *The Charisma Code* with your timeless words for peace.

To Tony Hsieh and your team at Zappos. You are experts in collaboration, efficiency, vision, flexibility, creativity, empowerment, and engagement. In other words, you are truly what you preach. Tony, your words change culture. Thank you for offering them to this book's humble cover.

To Michael Wall, for helping me turn *The Charisma Code* into a live and engaging seminar/workshop. Your mastery with groups is like nothing I've seen before.

To my publishers, Steve Scholl and Steve Sendar at White Cloud Press. What a journey! Thank you. This is actually just the beginning, isn't it?

To Justin Loeber, Nadine Hachicho, and Stephen Francy at Mouth Public Relations: Thank you for having a vision for me and this book that you care fiercely about. I love your big mouth!

To Joy DiBenedetto, another true global citizen of our day. I have one word for you . . . HUM.

To Scott Kuhagen for being the first to practice the Charisma Code and share the transformative effects its had on your life. *Bonus*—I get to be a major part of that life! May we always "seek to understand," together.

To my strong Grammy and my charismatic Bopie, who passed during the writing of this book: What you taught *lives* . . .

To my friend William Korthof, who also met death during this writing: May your revolutionary spirit inform those brave enough to *care*.

And to those I call my Fire family: You give me a circular dirt playground with a fire in the middle, and *so* much more. To you I sing these words directly: *"We only see how far we can go by virtue of the giants on whose shoulders we stand."*

And finally,
to my readers—thank you.
An art piece is never complete
until its audience appears.

ROBIN SOL LIEBERMAN

is a speaker, author and the founder of TrueCharisma. Using TrueCharisma's Global Communication Training program, she helps leaders, international companies, university students, refugees, ex-offenders, and anyone else whose lives improve when they learn to connect with people very different than themselves. With degrees in cultural anthropology, biomimicry, and performing arts, Robin brings a wealth of tools and experience to growing leaders, growing companies, and growing individuals as they learn to use their charisma to engage anyone in the world.

Dedicated to the emerging culture of the global citizen, Robin has spoken at the United Nations Headquarters, worked with global leaders through events organized by the Japanese Ministry of Foreign Affairs, with new arrival immigrants and refugees, and with the marketing teams of international companies such as Pfizer. She leads training sessions for IMPACT Leadership 21's Emerging Global Leaders program and serves as an advisor to Alliance 4 Empowerment, an organization committed to creating social and economic inclusion worldwide.

Robin brings her media background to social change. She has produced, directed, and starred in numerous TV and radio shows. As a celebrity interviewer, researcher, and observer of *Homo sapiens*, Robin will tell you she has learned most everything she knows from asking questions. To learn more about Robin and her business, please visit www.TrueCharisma.com.

The era of global citizenship is here. Learn to communicate in your language beyond words.

Discover more about your charisma code at

TrueCharisma
.com

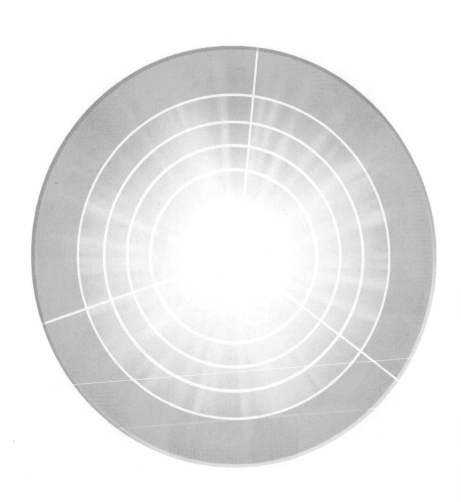